Lured by the seductions of power, wealth, and fame, many of our leaders have failed us, spreading waves of cynicism and distrust in their wake. Amid a culture that appears to be drowning, David Spickard draws on deep biblical truths and his vast personal experiences to provide hope and direction for all who are called to be a just leader. This is a profoundly important book for such a time as this.

—Brian Fikkert, Founder of the Chalmers Center at Covenant College and co-author of When Helping Hurts: How to Alleviate Poverty without Hurting the Poor . . . and Yourself

This is an insightful must-read for any business leader who wants to have a meaningful impact. It provides the needed foundations to navigate the cultural complexities of today's world with a refreshing and centered perspective while avoiding the traps of moral posturing. The message is both clear and simple and layered and complex: Seek justice, and the city will rejoice.

—Timothy J. Spence, CEO, BSA LifeStructures

I have long admired David Spickard's wisdom and the patient way he invites others to engage tough social issues. This biblically rich yet accessible book will help you gain the skills you need to navigate the complex pressures of this cultural moment. Through case studies, personal anecdotes, and actionable principles, David reminds readers that the path to justice is a path that leads all to a flourishing life. While valuable for individual readers, this book will be even more impactful if read with friends, fellow leaders, or in church small groups.

—Joanna Meyer, Founder, Women, Work, & Calling

The Just Leader will empower readers to lead with justice, mercy, and humility by examining their assumptions, biases, and blind spots and engaging in honest conversation, healthy introspection, and courageous action. This timely and significant work is filled with practical tools and guidance for leaders who want to create cultures and organizations that reflect God's heart for justice—just as author David Spickard has done throughout his career.

—Peter Greer, President & CEO, HOPE International, and coauthor of Rooting for Rivals

Christian leaders have a responsibility to lead toward the vision of flourishing outlined throughout our Scriptures and culminating in the life of Jesus. *The Just Leader* serves as a rebuttal to typical leadership guru shortcuts and sound bites, instead issuing a compelling and winsome invitation to join a journey of leaders who, like Zacchaeus, know they cannot simply continue in the old ways. Something newer and better is on offer, if we are willing to do the work.

—Jared Korver, CPA, CFP®, CEO, Beacon Wealthcare

David Spickard is one of the finest leaders today, helping others navigate a culturally complex landscape. For decades, he has meaningfully and thoughtfully engaged leaders across America on what holistic, relevant, and impactful leadership should and could look like. Forging a fair and impactful path is challenging. *The Just Leader* offers refreshingly practical wisdom.

—DJ Hill, Healthcare CEO

Over almost a decade of working with business leaders and pastors around issues of leadership and the integration of their Christian faith, I continually see people, myself included, struggle with confronting systems and processes that hurt others. This is especially true around matters of race. The Christian call to mercy and justice in Micah and throughout the New Testament requires us to not only care about this topic, but also to act. David has the hands-on experience with leaders of large and small companies to point us to relationship, excellence, and Christlike solutions. His work, while undergirded with theology, is not heady. Rather, it is searingly practical in a way that will make leaders uncomfortable in the best way, including me.

—Missy Wallace, Former Executive Director Global Faith &
Work Initiative at Redeemer City to City

David seems to find the most purposeful words to describe and dissect the complex and soul searching issues that leaders face under the surface of day-to-day "fire drills." As a leader seeking to align values with our practices, I find David's words a meaningful and practical guide. *The Just Leader* is also written in a riveting way; I wanted to both ponder over every page as well as speed-read the entire book! I value David's experience and wisdom, and his written communication of deep ideas is ideal to digest.

—Rob Burlington, SteelFab—Region President

For those leaders who want to do more than create a successful business or organization—the ones who set out to make wrong things right wherever they find them, who have the courage to tackle the human issues that go beyond the job description—David Spickard is the humble, thoughtful guide you need.

—Ross Chapman, CEO, Denver Institute for Faith & Work

It is time for Christian business leaders to start having open and honest conversations about true biblical justice and the role business can play in righting systemic injustice. *The Just Leader* gives business leaders the opportunity to do just that. David has masterfully articulated God's heart for justice and gives a practical guide on how leaders can apply the Scriptures to their work. It is a must-read for any leader who desires to make a true impact in their work and community.

—LaToya King, Chief Operations Officer,
Triangle Community Foundation

The Just Leader is a transformative masterpiece that beautifully captures the essence of true leadership. Grounded in the timeless wisdom of Jesus's words, "If the tree is good, the fruit will be good," this book unveils the profound truth that a just leader can create a world where life thrives for all. Spickard's profound insights illustrate how just leaders positively impact the lives of those around them, fostering flourishing communities within cities. With acute awareness, he guides leaders through the complexities of today's world, empowering them with cultural competence in leadership, race, economics, and gender identity as they ardently strive to shape a more equitable and just society.

—Eric Swanson, Senior Fellow, Leadership Network,
and co-author of To Transform a City

The Just Leader provides a clear framework for any leader interested in impactful community engagement. David has clearly and courageously weaved together easy to read stories that express what is possible when we live life from a redemptive lens. David has given us a go-to manual that will become timeless for the justice conscious leader!

—Pastor Ken Jenkins, Refuge and Restoration Church

The Just Leader comes at an opportune time as leaders increasingly face dilemmas at the crossroads of faith, culture, and organizational dynamics. It is a leadership imperative to not only know these just principles, but to also build your personal and organization principles and practices that are well informed, prayerful and strategic.

—Jon Mills, Senior VP of Operations

David's book helped me debunk some misunderstandings I had about what it meant to be "righteous" and gave me words and Scripture that enhanced my understanding of biblical justice. I found that the justice orientation that God had called me to in ministry for so long was, in fact, what he has been calling his people to for millennia.

—Joy Currey, Founder of The CORRAL Riding Academy

The Just Leader is a book that every Christian businessperson needs to buy. We're living in an age of deep division, and business leaders are often pressed with making decisions around contentious issues without having the tools to do so with wisdom. David Spickard has written a guide to help not only navigate these issues, but truly become the kind of leader for whom "the city rejoices" because they are blessing the city through their influence. This book is the standard bearer on faith, work, justice, and business.

—Jeff Haanen, Author of Working from the Inside Out

The Just Leader is courageous and timely. Issues of justice are tough to navigate, and David has gifted us a playbook. If you care deeply about people and your community, add this book to your required reading list.

—Ryan Ray, Former President and CEO of Jobs for Life

David Spickard writes from a perspective of not just head knowledge, but hands-on experience. He is and has been a just leader. This book will give any leader tried-and-true tools and wisdom to operate in midst of the fracture.

—Beverly Jenkins, CEO, Refuge and Restoration Ministries

David mentors the reader from practiced experience in an important but under-resourced realm of leadership development. His clear, accessible voice reads quickly and guides practically— there are no theoretical abstractions here. His business stories and metaphors make otherwise complex justice concepts tactile and applicable. In a "Physician, heal thyself!" spirit, David asks us to do needed interior and interpersonal work before diving first into perceived responses of justice (e.g., "What do I need to see?" before "What do I need to do?")

—Brian Gray, Fellowship Director, CityGate

The Just Leader does an incredible job of tackling the tough issues surrounding just leadership in our lighting-paced, ever-changing world. This book offers pragmatic insight into how business leaders can effectively cross socioeconomic lines and build meaningful relationships that positively integrate social capital into the fabric of their business. It is an eminently practical guide for both the inexperienced and experienced leader who is searching for creative and innovative ways to inculcate biblical justice into their corporation. *The Just Leader* strikes a balance between the tension of creating fairness and equity while helping the business owner not compromise their bottom line. One of the best books on just leadership written by a man who practices what he preaches. His unique methodologies simply work!

—Phillip Walker, Senior Pastor, Mt. Pleasant Worship & Outreach Center

I love this book: incredibly for-real, practical, and nuanced help for first-chair leaders to navigate the overwhelming array of complex leadership questions coming at us with dizzying speed. We hear constantly what NOT to do or say or think, but we need help for how to care, lead, speak, navigate. Thank you, David!

—Geoff Bradford, Sr. Pastor, Christ the King
Presbyterian Church, Raleigh, North Carolina

THE JUST LEADER

Thriving in a Fractured World

David Spickard

Cover design: Chelsey Malinaric

ISBN: 979-8-9892539-1-3 (softcover)
ISBN: 979-8-9892539-2-0 (hardcover)
ISBN: 979-8-9892539-0-6 (ebook)

Printed in the United States of America

5 4 3 2 1

CONTENTS

Good books, it is said, read us. They engender reflection and help us along a journey of self-discovery. This is one of those books. All of us long to live in a flourishing community and work in a flourishing workplace. Organizational leaders, over time, come to realize the outsized impact their convictions, language, and decisions have on shaping our workplaces and communities. They realize, too, that their words and actions are tested for consistency and impact. Does the walk match the talk? Do they reconcile?

This is a book about reconciliation. Not a reconciliation between people or groups. It is about a reconciliation between what you do every day and what, I suspect, you believe to be true and right in our communities on issues of mutual respect, shared prosperity, and thriving culture.

In these pages, David Spickard walks us through a study of God's own just character and unpacks sturdy principles of biblical justice. Enlarging on these themes, David invites leaders to see, build, give, and then act where injustice intersects our lives. David offers here a path forward for leaders: part biblical imperative, part field guide. Building on the important work of others, he blends his experience as a successful nonprofit practitioner with the understanding of a corporate director. This is no mere academic treatment of complex social justice topics. In these chapters, he frames the issues, points the way, and provides tools and stories to help leaders navigate their own terrain.

These are difficult and thorny topics. The tendency toward hand-wringing is strong. We fear that the leadership risk in stepping forward is not worth it. For those of us in the business community, it is much easier to simply keep our head down and focus on the next deal, the next investor, the next opportunity. The economic signals that help us keep score in the game are so familiar. It's much easier to let issues of justice and community flourishing stay in the lane of the nonprofit—those other people who are conversant in these matters. We'll cheer from the bleachers.

And yet, the complex issues of racial justice, human sexuality, broad access to capital, and systematic inequality tend to spill over into the work we do, the organizations we lead, and the people we work with. None of this is easy. As leaders, the invitation in these pages is to think and act well beyond mere financial philanthropy. It is an invitation to get out onto the field and learn to use our voice, our position, and our influence in new ways to bring about steadfast flourishing for everyone in the community.

Effective leaders understand that good decision-making begins with who is invited to the deliberation. Who's in the room? What voices and perspectives do they represent? Are there voices in the room that have a different perspective than mine? The best leaders understand that this is how progress is improved and poor decisions are avoided.

Over the past ten years, I have had the privilege of engaging with David on several justice-related issues. Not only has my thinking been sharpened through these conversations, but my courage has been bolstered, and my resolve to act has been strengthened.

To have faith means to do something. It's never enough simply to believe something. In these chapters, you will be invited to reflect on the roots of biblical justice and on what you can do as a leader to bring about a more just community. What resources over which you have influence can be employed in this work? What networks or relationships do you have that can be influential in this endeavor? Even if it means moving the needle only one degree toward enduring biblical justice, the encouragement of these pages will strengthen willing and reflective leaders.

—Craig Stephenson, President and CEO, COC Properties

Colt 45s and Lottery Tickets

Craig had a problem. As CEO of his family business, committed to creating value for his customers and impact for the communities in which his company operated, he was discouraged to hear the news about one of his company's convenience stores.

Located in a low-income neighborhood in a large metropolitan city, the store not only had become a site of local drug deals, but its highest-selling products were Colt 45 malt liquors and lottery tickets.

As a person of faith leading a company whose primary goal was to transform the lives of those it touched, Craig was crestfallen. This was not the transformation he was looking for.

So, he and his family members got to work. They determined their store needed to be razed, completely torn down. No longer would it be a place to attract this kind of activity. They embarked on a comprehensive strategy to completely remake the store, starting from the ground up: a new look, upgraded facilities, healthy food and beverage options, attractive landscaping, updated signage, bright colors—the works. The company wanted to invest in the community and demonstrate value to its residents by sparing no expense to have a flagship store providing products and services that would benefit everyone.

In the end, they invested over $1 million dollars to overhaul the store.

Craig and his family were proud to do their part, not only to improve their business, but to do so in a way that impacted lives in the community.

Or so they thought.

After months of operating the new store, they were dumbfounded to discover what the top selling products were . . .

Colt 45 malt liquors, lottery tickets, and drug deals.

LEADERSHIP CHALLENGE

Leaders face extraordinary challenges today. Not only are they tasked with carrying out the mission and vision of their businesses—a tough task in its own right. But contemporary leaders also need the skill to invest in and build up their people, achieve profitability, compete in the marketplace, and navigate growing social and cultural issues impacting their companies and communities.

Leading has never been an easy road. But in our post-pandemic world, the road gets more and more complicated by the day. Leaders are tired, burned out, exhausted. They are often needing quick fixes just to keep their heads above water, but instead the problems before them require an extra measure of insight, patience, wisdom, and strength.

Craig and his leaders understood how to retrofit a new store. Sure, that took a lot of work. Yes, it was expensive. But it was easy. Simple. Straightforward. What wasn't as straightforward was figuring out how to navigate the complex social context in which their business problem needed to be solved. And like many leaders, they didn't know what they didn't know until *after* they had tried to solve the problem.

Craig isn't the only one. Many leaders today haven't developed the skill to navigate the ever-evolving complexities of their social context. Like Craig, they have a ton of talent, insight, and resources. They can do *a lot*. But they don't know what they don't know. As a result, they are not thriving.

So much was under the surface for Craig, either unseen or misunderstood: the history of the community, relationships of trust with community leaders who could offer solutions and guide the path forward, the cultural, racial, and economic dynamics at play. Business leaders often don't have the time or foresight to pay attention to these issues. Instead, we do what we do best . . . come in with our own solutions.

But if our solutions are only making problems worse for others and even ourselves, maybe it's time we take a step back and ask some probing questions.

- *What are we, as leaders, not seeing?*
- *How did we get to this point?*
- *What do we need to learn?*
- *With whom do we need to spend time to deepen our understanding?*
- *How can we thrive and help our people and communities thrive?*
- *And what does any of this have to do with being* just?

WHY I'M WRITING THIS BOOK—AND WHY YOU'RE READING IT

I'm assuming that if you've picked up this book, you care enough to seek solutions to the big problems in our society. You want to see communities transformed. You want to see people thriving. You yourself want to thrive. And you want the world to be a better place because of your involvement in it. In short, while you may not have realized this, you want to be a leader who is characterized by *justice*.

I'm also assuming that—like Craig—you realize this is no easy task. You're looking for a guide. And it's also safe to assume that just like many of us, you're just plain tired.

Moreover, *justice* is a very thorny word. It comes with lots of baggage as it's been defined and redefined by our society. Many of us don't want to touch it with a ten-foot pole. To be completely honest, I'm with you. I feel lost, confused, and frustrated every time I engage in conversations about business, leadership, and what it looks like to navigate issues of justice.

As a leader of faith coming from a worldview centered on the Bible, I find it extremely difficult to wade through these waters. These weren't conversations I had growing up as a White kid in my predominantly White church. Rarely, if ever, did we talk about justice. And there certainly wasn't any formal teaching or training on the topic.

This book, therefore, is an attempt to provide for you what I never had. Writing as a follower of Jesus and pulling out principles from Scripture and Jesus's life, my hope is that whether you come from a faith background or not, you will find the guidance in this book to be helpful and hopeful. That you will see the central role justice has to play in leadership. That you will come to learn, as I have, that the path to justice is also your path to a thriving, flourishing life. That because of this book you will thrive, your people will thrive, and your community will thrive.

If you are a business leader (particularly a White business leader) who's wondering what role you can play, you've picked up the right book. Business, after all, has to play a part. But in my experience, White business leaders can be reluctant to engage in conversations about justice.

Why? From the business leaders' perspective, the conversations can be too messy. People involved in community work rarely understand business, so it's like speaking a completely different language. Plus, every time business leaders engage in these issues, they can feel attacked, as if *they* are the problem. So they take a step back.

The result? Business leaders are more isolated from the community's problems. Some give up engaging, resorting to building their bottom line. Some try to keep doing good work in the community, but their distance from the problems means their solutions aren't addressing the core issues.

But here's the kicker: These issues are not just out in the community. They are showing up in their businesses and organizations every day. Like Craig's dilemma, business leaders and other leaders of influence are having to engage in what I would call "just issues" on a regular basis that require an extra layer of insight, wisdom, and expertise they haven't needed before. And if they don't know how to address them, they and their companies will be left behind.

At this point, many leaders may be tempted to just throw in the towel and pine for the "good old days" when leadership was simpler. When the world felt simpler. But we can't go back. And if you're reading this book for the same reason I'm writing it, you suspect there just might be a better way forward. A way where everyone experiences what it means to thrive (including you!)

There is.

HEALING FOR A FRACTURED WORLD

Our world is crying out for justice. And many of us struggle to know how to navigate that. On the coattails of a global pandemic, political divisiveness, racial unrest, and a general feeling of anger and discontentment, issues related to justice are at the forefront.

We've been pummeled by the fractured world around us, with highly emotional words and opinions coming from all sides, calling out both individual and systemic injustices and the ways we have failed one another. It all feels too broken to know where to start. Leaders are left wondering what in the world to do.

Despite the long presence of injustice in our world, many of us struggle to know how to be just leaders in our businesses and communities. Many leaders like me have real questions:

- *What is justice anyway and why should I even care?*
- *I'm tired of feeling blamed for injustice. Issues are much more complicated than they appear. Don't people see the risks I've taken and the good that's been accomplished?*
- *I feel guilty when I see injustice, but I don't know what to do. What if I say or do the wrong thing? Will I get canceled? Isn't it just easier not to say or do anything?*
- *How should I think about the money I have? How much is enough? What is the best way to use it to be just?*
- *Why do we have to keep talking about race? We want to have more racial diversity, but it's not that easy.*

- *What about Diversity Equity and Inclusion (DEI)? I know we should create a workplace that's equitable, but where do we even start?*
- *How does being just inform the way we pay our people, treat our customers, and impact our community?*
- *I want to be just, but I also need to compete and be profitable. How is it even possible to do both at the same time?*

For lots of us, what we're hearing are new ideas, concepts, and history we have never been exposed to before and perspectives that challenge what we believe to be true or normal. Often, we question people's agendas and why they feel the way they do.

Sometimes, we feel guilty that we're unaware and even made to feel shame because we are seen as the source of the injustice. Other times, we're deeply frustrated by people making blanket statements with strong opinions we do not agree with. We don't like having "our side" of the story depicted so negatively and (we believe) unfairly. Conversations about these topics go nowhere, often creating more frustration, disagreement, and anger. So, we avoid them at all costs and dismiss those with whom we do not agree.

At least, we're tempted to.

As we survey the fractures in our world—and, more importantly, in our community—we leaders have a choice to make. We can try to avoid these issues. But if we do, they'll just keep coming up. The brokenness will keep coming for us—in our workplaces, our neighborhoods, our churches, our schools, and even our homes.

Or we can become agents of healing in a fractured world.

We can chart a new way forward.

We can pay attention to issues we've overlooked before.

We can develop both the skill and the understanding to read our social contexts.

We can learn to provide real and lasting solutions.

We can be leaders who are known for justice. Because we'll have learned a piece of ancient wisdom: Leaders thrive by being just. In the end, there's only one road from fractured to flourishing.

The road to justice and the road to thriving . . . are one.

CHAPTER 1

Life in the Bubble

Chris Mangum was senior vice president of his family's business, CC Mangum, a heavy highway construction company in Raleigh, North Carolina, started by his grandfather in the early 1900s. Well respected in the community, Chris loved the way his business allowed him to carry on the legacy of hard work and loyalty that had defined his father and grandfather. He had a passion for working with heavy construction equipment, and his office displayed miniature scale models he obtained from equipment distributors.

Chris was frequently entrenched in the day-to-day demands of running a business and being a good steward of his time to his family and community. He would receive information about countless events going on in the community and felt guilty not attending more of them. One invitation had been sitting on his desk for many weeks, perched on top of a stack of papers.

This was a special invitation to hear a man named Dr. John Perkins speak. Dr. Perkins was born into material poverty in Mississippi, the son of a sharecropper. He grew up in the racially divided South and, as a young African American, experienced firsthand the horrors of injustice.

Dr. Perkins's outspoken support and leadership role in civil rights demonstrations resulted in repeated harassment, imprisonment, and beatings. Birthed from these experiences, he became one of the leading voices to come out of the American civil rights movement, and he was speaking at a community gathering in Raleigh.

Due to the demands of his business, Chris couldn't attend but instead sent his brother, Merl, in his place. Merl was so captivated by the experience that he stayed after the event and waited for a recording of the talk. Cassette tape in hand (yes, that's dating this story), he rushed back to the office and told Chris, "You have to listen to this."

Chris ignored the tape for weeks. But then, one day, he had to travel out of town to visit a job site. The thought occurred to him, *Why not give the tape a try?* So, on the way out of his office, he picked up the cassette tape and popped it into his truck stereo system. If nothing else, it would make the drive go by a little quicker.

That one small decision would change the course of Chris's life.

Halfway into his trip, Chris could not focus on anything except the words coming from the speakers of his truck. He almost forgot where he was going. The demands of his day and the needs of the job site faded into the distance as he listened intently to Dr. Perkins.

Dr. Perkins's story is profound. He didn't just live through the experience of the racially divided South; he became a leader and paid the price for his leadership. Even though Chris's own experience was radically different, he could not ignore the pain.

It wasn't just the injustice that Chris felt deep in his heart; it was the forgiveness and mercy that Dr. Perkins freely gave to his abusers. He didn't focus on oppression and pain. Instead, he talked about hope and healing. He spoke of Jesus, the one who took on our suffering so we could be free to serve as agents of justice and mercy in our neighborhoods and communities, advocates for the brokenhearted, poor, outcast, and forgotten. Chris could feel the passion in Dr. Perkins's words as if he were sitting right beside him.

With tears welling up in his eyes, Chris realized he was missing out on the fullness of God by living a life isolated from those around him who were still experiencing oppression—not just out in the community but even within his own company. He never planned to turn his back on his neighbors and miss the deep meaning God intended for his life. He didn't realize he was too busy for God. As Chris began to inventory his life, he realized there was no one around him who was different than him. With Christ's life as a representation, Chris realized he was living life in a bubble.

As Chris continued to digest the words of Dr. Perkins, he questioned everything: his attitudes, his experiences, his work, his choices, his friends, his values, even his faith. He wondered how he could have let this happen. Why did he feel so lonely as a leader? How did he become so insulated from the brokenness and needs of others? How did he not have any deep, meaningful relationships with those of a different race and life experience? What could he do to make it right?

Something had to change. He just didn't know how.

Chris confided in a close friend about his struggle. His friend challenged him with one simple idea: "If you want to engage people different from you, particularly people of color, you must first develop a meaningful relationship with *one* person of color."

To Chris, that seemed impossible.

THE PARKING LOT

Pastor Donald McCoy had never heard of CC Mangum, but the recommendation from a member of his congregation was all he needed. He gave CC Mangum a call to see if he could get an estimate.

Typically, when someone calls CC Mangum, they first speak with the main receptionist who directs calls to the appropriate person. Unless someone has already had direct contact with Chris, there are usually two or three people who respond to incoming calls before reaching Chris. For some reason, that didn't happen on this particular day.

When Chris's phone rang on his desk, he answered it, knowing only important calls were getting through that day. Upon picking up the receiver, he heard a voice he did not recognize.

"Hello, is this CC Mangum?" the caller asked.

Chris was surprised. Usually the person on the line was his secretary, Janet. She would tell him who was calling and then patch the caller in. Why was someone else on the line asking if this was CC Mangum?

Chris courteously responded, "Yes, this is CC Mangum; can I help you?"

The caller replied, "Hello, this is Pastor Donald McCoy, and I am the pastor of Pleasant Hill United Church of Christ. Our church parking lot needs to be paved, and I would like to get an estimate."

At first, Chris didn't know what to do. Normally, in this situation, he would direct Pastor McCoy to one of CC Mangum's project managers who would assess the project, find a time to meet with the customer, survey the land, and develop an estimate.

But something made him stay on the line. Chris sensed this was no ordinary call and no ordinary project. There was a reason this call came directly to him.

"Pastor McCoy, we would be happy to see if we can help you."

Then Chris decided, against all his usual protocol, to visit the site himself.

When Chris arrived at Pleasant Hill, Pastor McCoy and one of the church's trustees, Minister McCotter, greeted him. Pastor McCoy was about ten years older than Chris, had a mustache, and looked similar in size. He was bi-vocational, serving full time as pastor of Pleasant Hill and full time as an environmental chemist for the state of North Carolina. He was the only African American chemist working in the state office.

With his silver hair, muscular build, and glasses, Chris had a regal look about him. People often thought he was older than his actual age. Regardless of the temperature, he always wore a short-sleeved shirt with the CC Mangum logo over his heart.

Pleasant Hill was on a long country road about ten miles south of Raleigh. Built in 1913, the building was a typical country church with space for worship and a few small rooms for Sunday school. The grassy, gravel area next to the church served as the parking lot. It was uneven, full of potholes and tire tread marks from years of use. Pastor McCoy showed Chris the area where he wanted the paving to be done, and Chris began walking the lot with his measuring wheel.

While he measured, Chris focused intently on his work, making sure to recall all he knew about measuring a parking lot. The work wasn't difficult, but he wanted to be precise.

Within close earshot, Chris kept getting distracted by Pastor McCoy's conversation with Minister McCotter. He could hear them talking about the goodness of the Lord, God's work in their lives, and the ways he had demonstrated his faithfulness to them. Their talk wasn't contrived; it was as normal as if they were talking about last night's football game. God was not only real for them, he was actively working in their lives—and his presence was palpable, as if the Lord was standing right beside them.

Chris wondered if he had that type of relationship with God. He had been a Christian all his life, but he rarely talked like this—normal conversation peppered with words describing God's active work. Chris did not expect to be convicted about his faith in God while measuring a parking lot. Then again, he didn't exactly know what he was expecting from this job; he just somehow knew he was supposed to be at this place at this time.

After about fifteen minutes or so, Chris finished his measurements and told Pastor McCoy he had the information he needed to complete the estimate. Pastor McCoy thanked him for his time but asked him not to leave yet. There was still one more thing they needed to do.

Pastor McCoy invited Chris into the church. They entered the sanctuary, and Pastor McCoy and Minister McCotter proceeded to the front of the sanctuary, where they knelt down face-first on the steps of the altar. Chris stood in the aisle at the back of the church, waiting to see what they wanted. When he saw them lying prostrate, he didn't know what to do—that is, until Pastor McCoy looked back at him and motioned for Chris to join them up front.

Chris slowly walked down the aisle, feeling a bit of nerves creeping into his stomach, and carefully took his place face-first between the two men. Pastor McCoy began to pray for the parking lot. He asked God to be Lord over it, to provide for it, to bless Chris and CC Mangum. He thanked God for sending Chris and his gifts to help them with this project, and he asked God to allow them to trust him for all things.

As Chris listened, his mind went back to Dr. Perkins's talk and the challenge he had received from his friend. If he was ever to engage people of color, he first needed to have a relationship with one person of color. He realized right then they weren't just praying for a parking lot—they were praying for a friendship.

Pastor McCoy didn't know if he would ever see Chris again after they prayed together at the front of his church's sanctuary. When Chris responded with the estimate—$11,000—it was well above the church's budget for the project, making it impossible for Pastor McCoy to choose CC Mangum for the work. Pastor McCoy was at a loss for what he should do.

So he did what he always did: He took the information back to the congregation . . . and they prayed.

When Chris gave Pastor McCoy the amount of the estimate, he anticipated it would be too steep for the church. But he couldn't just forget about it. He was torn between the needs of his business and his deep desire to serve Pastor McCoy and his ministry, so he proactively made some phone calls.

After a few days of work, Chris called Pastor McCoy. Several of CC Mangum's vendors had responded to Chris's calls, agreeing to offer significant discounts on their materials and services for the project. In addition, the leaders at CC Mangum decided to contribute some of their *own* money toward the parking lot. All of these gifts reduced the estimate significantly—as in from $11,000 to *one hundred dollars.*

CC Mangum ended up paving Pleasant Hill's parking lot for one hundred dollars. Yes, one hundred dollars.

But more than that, Pastor McCoy and Chris became close friends.

They decided to meet every Wednesday at Crowley's Restaurant to have lunch together. They hardly missed a week.

And then, one day, those lunches would begin to impact a whole lot more people—including me.

THE GOAL: FIND SIX JOBS

"Donald, we can't find drivers for our trucks. And every day those trucks sit parked, we're losing thousands of dollars."

During one of their weekly lunches, Chris asked Pastor McCoy for prayer. CC Mangum could not find good workers to drive their trucks. Finding good workers to meet the needs of their business was a common challenge for many companies. Pastor McCoy said he would pray, but he had an additional response.

He said, "You know what, Chris? There are able-bodied men and women in my church and in my neighborhood who are parked—just like your trucks—because they don't have a job. They stand out on Hargett Street all day, idle with nothing to do. They come to my Sunday morning service, homeless, unemployed, and underemployed, and no matter how hard I preach the good news of the Gospel to them, they walk out of my church homeless, unemployed, and underemployed. They come to me and say, 'Pastor, I need a job.' But I don't know where to send them."

In that moment, Chris and Pastor McCoy realized they each had something the other needed.

Chris had jobs. Pastor McCoy had people.

Surely, they could figure out a way to help each other.

After their lunch at Crowley's, Chris and Pastor McCoy each committed to invite twelve of their friends to gather at Ballentine's Restaurant to hear their idea. One by one, pastors and businesspeople began to arrive. They didn't know exactly what to expect, but each of them had decided to come because of the invitation they had received from Chris and Pastor McCoy.

Since Chris only knew White businesspeople, and Pastor McCoy only knew Black pastors, the group in the room was quite diverse.

None of the invited guests had ever experienced anything like this. Rarely did pastors and businesspeople do anything together. Both apprehension and anticipation filled the room. While some knew of each other, most had never met. And yet when Pastor McCoy and Chris began to speak, the group quickly realized the significance of the moment.

Chris and Pastor McCoy shared their story, what brought them together, and what they believed God was doing through their relationship. They shared the conversation they had at Crowley's and the aha moment they experienced when they realized each had something the other needed.

They wondered out loud what it could look like if pastors and business leaders in the city not only served one another but helped those in their community who were struggling to find work. They didn't know where this might lead but thought if they had the same needs, maybe others did too.

Pastor McCoy and Chris's words were like a spark. One by one, people began to speak. Each person expressed the same concerns and affirmed Chris and Pastor McCoy's vision. At first, they didn't know exactly what to do next, but the more they talked, the more it became quite clear what they could do together: *Let's help six people find jobs*. That was the goal—simple, doable, and impactful. If nothing else comes of this, the group would have done something worthwhile by helping six people get jobs.

At that point, one of the businessmen raised his hand and said, "How about we start right now? I have a job I need to fill today."

After describing the position, one of the pastors jumped in and said, "I know the perfect person for that job."

Pretty soon, more matches began to take place through the connections the group was making with one another.

Over the course of the next month, they found jobs for fifteen people, far exceeding the goal they had set for themselves.

There was just one problem. They found it was easy to help people *find* jobs. But they soon discovered it was something entirely different to help them *keep* those jobs.

BEYOND JOBS

Chris, Pastor McCoy, and the group of pastors and business leaders began to notice that many of the people they had placed in jobs had significant barriers in their lives—both physical and emotional—making it virtually impossible for them to stay committed and faithful to their work.

Many had a spotty work history, a lack of positive role models, a prison record, no transportation, poor work ethic, no child care, and very little education. Circumstances in their lives had led some to have a victim mentality, a disrespect for authority, and no desire to work.

A job alone couldn't fix what was going on. Something was broken on the inside of these individuals that had to be addressed before they were able to have success at work (let alone at life).

To tackle this issue, the group decided they needed to do two things: 1) teach people what God says about work, and 2) provide everyone with a mentor. Doing so would not only help people find and keep jobs, but also get to the root issues keeping them from being the men and women they were created to be.

Their simple idea became what is now Jobs for Life (JfL), a global organization based in Raleigh, equipping people all over the country and even internationally to learn God's design for work and connect them to a community of people who can help them find and keep meaningful employment.

What was intended for just six people is now helping thousands of men, women, and families per year, as JfL classes are currently being held in urban and suburban churches, prisons, halfway houses, YMCAs, ministries to at-risk children, homeless shelters, substance abuse treatment centers, and countless other nonprofit ministries. Businesses are gaining access to a pool of qualified employees to meet their needs. And communities are being transformed as church, business, and civic leaders are working together to provide a solution to joblessness in their cities.

Chris and Pastor McCoy never imagined such an outcome from their relationship with each other.

As a business leader, Chris was unsure how to act on the feelings he experienced from listening to Dr. Perkins's talk. After all, he was consumed with the needs of his business and hardly had time for much else. But he did recognize his need, prayed for the Lord to meet his need, and took steps to move out of his bubble even when doing so didn't make sense.

Same with Pastor McCoy—the Lord was working in him as well. He had never had a relationship with someone like Chris before, and he took a risk to pursue him. In his experience, a relationship with a White business leader usually came with strings attached. But not with Chris, so he took steps out of his bubble to pursue and trust him, and the Lord did the rest.

In the end, not only were Chris and Pastor McCoy both thriving, but thousands of others were thriving as well. And it all began with a cassette tape.

I sometimes wonder, What if Chris hadn't sent Merl to hear Dr. Perkins? What if Merl didn't take the next step of picking up a tape? What if Chris hadn't listened to the cassette tape in his truck? What if Pastor McCoy hadn't called CC Mangum to get an estimate? What if his call didn't go straight to Chris's desk? What if Chris had delegated the job, as he nearly always did? What if Pastor McCoy didn't invite Chris in to pray after he measured the parking lot?

What if Chris and Pastor McCoy had allowed their fears to keep them separated? What if those weekly lunches never happened?

For one thing, the next twenty years of my life would have looked dramatically different.

QUESTIONS TO CONSIDER

1. What about Chris and Pastor McCoy's story resonates with you the most?
2. When you look at your life, what is keeping you from thriving?
3. Where do you feel like you are living in a bubble?
4. What steps can you take to move out of that bubble?

CHAPTER 2

Why Am I Here?

It was a cold, overcast Sunday morning. My wife, Alice, and I were scrambling as usual to get our young children ready for church. Mornings are not our best time of the day, particularly when our kids were especially young. And this Sunday was no different.

We had been blessed with two boys and a girl, and they had come one right after the other. Alice was pregnant with our fourth, and the other three were four years old and younger. *Survival* was the operative word. Sleep was a figment of our imagination. *Thriving* wasn't on our radar screen.

Being a light sleeper, I was usually up early before everyone else, while Alice slept a bit longer, with our kids waking up at random times. We did our best to ease into the day—me with my normal bowl of cereal and the sports page and Alice with precious moments of extra sleep. And yet, nine mornings out of ten, time got away from us, and we'd have to make a mad dash to get everyone dressed, in the car, and ready to go wherever we needed to go. We usually made it, but it was always close.

At the time, we were attending a small church plant. (*Plant* is a term that means new, or just launched from a larger church.) We had a core of about forty people, mostly in their twenties and thirties, with around twenty young children. While Alice and I knew being a part of a church plant would require some sacrifices, we were drawn to this particular one because of its deep commitment to teaching the Bible and a desire to serve poor people in the city. We did not know exactly what that meant, but Alice and I thought it was a great fit for our family.

That Sunday, when we arrived, we hastily found our normal seats toward the back of the room. We didn't notice those who were seated near us. Visitors trickled in from time to time each Sunday, but most were familiar faces. I failed to see the group sitting behind us—one man and three women—who were new to our church and looking somewhat out of place. It wasn't until halfway through the service when our pastor instructed us to stand and greet those around us that I met our new visitors. The man's name, I would soon learn, was Don. Little did I know how Don would soon change my life forever.

I grew up in Nashville, Tennessee, the youngest of three children. My sister and brother are nine and seven years older than me respectively, which was the best of both worlds for me—the experience of a big family with older siblings to look up to and learn from and the attention afforded to an only child once my brother and sister left for college.

I went to public schools through sixth grade and then attended and graduated from an elite all-boys academy for middle and high school. Sports always have been a deep interest of mine. Looking back, the affirmation and value I received from my athletic success was like a drug. I couldn't get enough of it.

I worshiped my older siblings. They actually wanted me around, which was huge for me. I would tag along with their friends, experiencing a level of cool only afforded to a ten-year-old who is welcomed and accepted by a group of high schoolers. Ah, the good old days.

My sister, Susan, has always been a constant source of strength and a picture of faithfulness to me. She taught me (or should I say strongly told me) to think of others first by asking them questions to find out how they are doing before talking about myself. I took that lesson to heart so much that I find it difficult even today to talk about myself comfortably.

My brother, Anderson, was my hero. He paved the way for me so that everywhere I went, people were drawn to me. Not because I was anything special, but simply because I was Anderson's little brother. Life was always better when he was around. So much so, I cried uncontrollably when he left for college and waited impatiently at the window every time he came home for a visit.

And my parents provided me with the constant love and faithfulness very few children experience. Once my brother left for college, we dubbed ourselves the Three Musketeers. Admittedly, my coolness factor dropped like a rock overnight once I became one of the Three Musketeers. But life was still good.

Mom took me everywhere, making sure I grew up with a combination of faith, well-roundedness, and a certain level of grit. For the well-rounded part, she surprised me one day when I was in second grade by picking me up early from school. On the front seat were my brand-new piano books waiting for my first piano lesson. Believe it or not, I loved it. I always had wanted to learn how to play the piano like my mom.

As for the grit, it was the little things—dropping me off far from school to have me walk the rest of the way instead of taking me to the school door like the other moms did, having me do my own laundry, and making sure I sent a handwritten thank you note whenever I received a gift (something I still do). My mom was on the board of directors of numerous nonprofit organizations in the city—from organizations that supported the public schools and inner-city ministries to the Girl Scouts. I believe I am still the only ten-year-old boy to have ever appeared in a Girl Scout parade. Not sure how I was to develop grit from that, but oh well.

From Dad, I learned a deep love for God and commitment to others. He spent practically all of his life as a physician and was an expert in the treatment of addiction. Dad was an "old-school" doctor with his black bag and stethoscope. I have distinct memories of watching him pick up his bag and walk out the front door after dinner to make yet another house call for one of his hundreds of patients. He was committed not only to their physical health but their emotional and spiritual health as well.

Most days, I'd hear him walking down the steps of our home early in the morning to go into his study to pray directly below my bedroom. I'd roll over to get a few more hours of sleep knowing my father was underneath me praying for me. He'd do all he could to make sure the people he cared for were well, especially us Spickards.

Growing up with such a family, it's difficult for me to imagine what it would be like not to have a family's love and affirmation. It was something I thought everyone had.

KUDZU VILLAGE

When Don and I met during the greeting time at church, he introduced me to the three women with him, and we exchanged small talk until the service began again. He was ruddy like me, with a fair complexion and red hair. I thought he might be five to ten years older than me, but it was difficult to pinpoint his age; he looked worn yet had a youthful spirit.

After the service was over, we talked some more and said our goodbyes. I expressed a desire to see him and his friends the next Sunday, not thinking they would actually come back.

To my amazement, they appeared the next Sunday—and many more Sundays after that. Don and his friends lived in a rooming house just down the street from our church, so it was convenient for him and the ladies to walk to church. He showed up faithfully, sometimes with his friends, sometimes not. The more Don came, the more we talked. The more we talked, the more we became friends and spent time together.

Don's home was affectionately called "Kudzu Village," an older, two-story structure near downtown that was home to around twenty people. The name came from the kudzu vines that covered much of the home's front exterior and sides. Whenever I had the chance, I would stop by Kudzu Village to see Don. Each time, I was taken by the smell of the home and the amount of people there during the day. It was like I had entered into an entirely new world unbeknownst to the houses and neighbors around them.

First, the smell—it hit me in the face every time I entered. It was like walking into a locker room full of stale, sweaty clothes. You couldn't get away from it.

And then there were all the people. No matter what time of day, people were there. Just there. Not really doing anything, just . . . existing. You'd open one bedroom and there would be three people hanging out, another room with five, another with two, and a few loners in the bunch. All passing the time away with no real plans and certainly no purpose. While I appreciated the opportunity to see into this new world, I became increasingly angry and frustrated by it. This is what people living on the dime looks like—government assistance at its best.

Don and I could not have been more different. He had led a life of much pain and struggle, had moved countlessly as a child, and had been disowned by his parents. He didn't think much of himself. Very few people in his life spoke to him of his value, and he had no real goal or purpose to achieve, no real dreams. Relationships did not come easy either, particularly those with women. His last one prior to our meeting was extremely abusive and led him into a dark, downward spiral.

After an ugly verbal fight with his (then) girlfriend, she kicked Don out of her car, and he was left with nowhere to go. He had no home and owned only the clothes on his back. Mad at the world, feeling abandoned, and wanting to distance himself as far as he possibly could from other people, Don began walking and ended up in the woods off a main highway on the outskirts of our city. That became his new home . . . *for the next year.*

When Don told me he had been homeless, he said he was "hardcore homeless." I didn't know exactly what he meant, but I got a sense of it the more he described what life looked like for him that year. With his previous military training, he dug a revetment in the woods to hide in during the day. Only at night would he come out and look for food and water in the dumpsters and businesses nearby. He was invisible.

Listening to him, I tried to imagine what it must have been like to live in a ditch . . . for a year . . . with no one else around. How does someone get to that point? Why would he hate people that much? How could he hate himself that much?

The more Don talked, the more I wondered how I could possibly relate to him. Invisible? Abandoned? Homeless? Hardly! All I knew was blessing, love, support, and affirmation.

And yet, there was something pulling at me to have a relationship with him. I didn't know why. From my perspective, we had nothing in common. To be honest, I was a little afraid of Don, and after all, I was up to my ears in diapers, overwhelmed with responsibility in my job, and just trying to get from one day to the next.

Moreover, Don did not look like he wanted to change, and quite honestly, I was frustrated with where he was. No matter his background, I wondered how someone could just exist with no purpose or drive. How could he not want more in a place to live? Where was his desire to work? Why would he just live on disability and be content depending on the government for his survival?

This would be a total waste of my time.

"SOMEONE WITH AN MBA"

On paper, few people would have been as qualified as me to engage Don effectively. I should have been ready. After all, I had just received my dream job: director of operations at a new nonprofit called Jobs for Life.

Even though I had grown up in privilege, I was always impacted by the ways Jesus gravitated toward those in need and called his followers to do the same. I began to realize caring for the poor was not optional for the Christian, but at the very core of what it means to be a Christian. Not just for those gifted to work with people in need. Or for the deacons. But for all of us, no matter what position or role we are in. For me, I wanted that to be my vocation. I wanted to lead a nonprofit organization specifically designed to engage the material poor.

To my surprise, when I sought counsel from older leaders and told them what I wanted to do, overwhelmingly they encouraged me to get my MBA. I was shocked. An MBA? Why? They responded by saying, "Nonprofits need leaders who understand business principles to help them operate with excellence."

And so, Alice and I packed our bags and moved to Bloomington, Indiana, where I got my MBA from Indiana University. During that time, I felt like a fish out of water. My reasons for being there were completely opposite from those of my classmates. I often came home from school having learned about stock swaps and derivatives, wondering with Alice what I was doing there. And yet, as it turned out, it was the perfect path and training I needed.

Except for one problem. No one told me that nonprofits don't recruit at MBA schools!

Lucky for me, consulting companies do—which led us to Birmingham, Alabama, where I got a job as a business analyst for a large consulting company. It was a job I appreciated but did not enjoy. It was extremely boring and not at all what I wanted to do, yet it ended up being the exact step I needed to take to lead me where I wanted to go.

Still holding out hope for a leadership position within a nonprofit, I randomly saw a flier at a church in Birmingham announcing a national conference coming to the city. I was not familiar with it, but it intrigued me. It was the Christian Community Development Association (CCDA), co-founded by . . . want to guess?

Dr. John Perkins.

I had never heard of Dr. Perkins or this organization, but during my years at MBA school, I had done an internship with a community development organization in Indianapolis. I never knew there was a Christian organization focused on community development.

So, I took a day off work and went to one day of the conference.

It was there I found what I had been looking for: a little nonprofit founded by a pastor and a businessman where churches and businesses in

Raleigh were working together to help unemployed and underemployed individuals get jobs.

I said to myself, "That's it! I found it."

This was the late 1990s, so there was no social media. But I did all I could to stalk Jobs for Life. I reached out to friends who happened to know Chris Mangum, and I cold-called him to introduce myself and let him know my interest in working for JfL. There were no positions, nor was there funding at the time, but he appreciated my call (or so he said).

I called Chris every six weeks or so to check in. I'd record and rerecord the perfect voicemail to leave on his company phone, searching for the exact words and tone to convince him and the other leaders I would be a real asset for their work. I took the JfL class and learned everything I could about what they were teaching. I even traveled to various cities and sat in the audience for their trainings. I was a JfL groupie!

After a year, they finally relented, probably because they got so tired of me. It turns out they received a grant that allowed them to fund a position for someone with a business background who could help JfL grow. They needed "someone with an MBA."

I couldn't think of anything better to do. Instead of just giving handouts to people in need, doesn't it make sense to help them learn the value of work, develop the attitude and skills companies need, and then connect them to jobs? It made perfect sense to me, so I dove in headfirst.

I served as director of operations for six years and then as CEO for twelve—eighteen years total. During that time, Jobs for Life grew from a local organization in Raleigh to having a presence in 450 cities and eight countries, helping leaders all over the world equip men and women to learn God's design for work and overcome the barriers people face in finding, keeping, and growing in their jobs.

It's hard to overestimate the impact JfL had on my life. I was mentored by extraordinary leaders who showed me a world I had no idea existed. I saw leaders not settle for living in their bubble and instead use their talents and resources to affect real change in their communities. I met people who overcame insurmountable odds to thrive at work and provide for themselves and their families. I visited communities that continually experience tragedy and brokenness because of poverty, crime, and injustice. And I saw people build the most unlikely of friendships, like Chris and Pastor McCoy's, through their common mission and desire to see their communities transformed.

It was here that I began to explore what it meant to be a just leader. What did it look like for followers of Jesus to engage the injustices in the world around them? How could we understand those injustices, get close to them, and understand more deeply why they were happening? How could we put politics aside and effectively navigate issues of justice when they were so polarizing, messy, and complicated? Why should we care—and did any of it even matter?

I wasn't an expert in justice then, and I'm not an expert in justice today. Being someone who is just is not a destination; it's a process. You're not unjust one day and then *poof*, you're just the next. It's a journey, a pursuit toward an ideal we ultimately will not obtain in this life. But it's a journey worth taking, marked by the fullness of God and his promises. It's ultimately a way for all of us to thrive.

I didn't know that when I started at Jobs for Life. But I know it now—because Don taught me.

DON'S KUDZU . . . AND MINE

Kudzu, the woody vine that gave Don's house its name, covers more than seven million acres of the deep South. The climate of the Southeastern United States is perfect for kudzu. The vines grow as much as a foot per day during the summer months, climbing trees, power poles, and anything else they come in contact with. Under ideal conditions, kudzu vines can grow sixty feet each year.

While they help prevent erosion, the vines destroy valuable forests by preventing trees from getting sunlight. As a result, lots of people are working hard to get rid of kudzu. The problem is that it grows too well. In order to get rid of it, scientists have found that herbicide treatments must be consistently applied for at least four years. But even with the most effective herbicides, some kudzu plants can take as long as ten years to kill.[1] Ten years!

From where I stood, the issues in Don's life grew as rapidly and uncontrollably as the kudzu that enveloped his home. Don spent entire days producing very detailed colored pencil drawings; they were graphic and gory, though admittedly extraordinary. As the drawings suggested, Don lived a life filled with fear. A self-described enemy of God, he was afraid of seeing himself beyond his current circumstances.

The solution for Don was not a quick fix. It would take years to cut back those issues in his life. And even after those years, it was highly possible that no progress would be made.

What I didn't realize at the time was that my issues were just as uncontrollable. My safe, privileged, Christian background made me think I was better than everyone else. In fact, more than that, I thought God thought I was better than everyone else. That God favored me because of the things I had.

You see, I can be deeply judgmental of others. It's not usually overt, but it's there. Deep inside, I measure people up based on the value I think they can provide for me. I could not see what a friendship with Don could offer to me. *It would be a sacrifice for me*, I thought. *If anything, Don is lucky I want to be his friend.*

Because of my pride, I struggle with having a deep dependency upon God, knowing I am nothing without him. It's so easy for me to anesthetize myself from needing him by pursuing the things I have to comfort me.

The solution for me was not a quick fix. It would take years to cut back those issues in my life. And even after those years, it was highly possible that no progress would be made.

Don and I both needed help, but we didn't know what to do next. Thankfully, there was a Jobs for Life class getting ready to begin at our church.

Despite his fears and my apprehension, Don agreed to take the class, and I agreed to be his mentor (a "champion" in Jobs for Life's language). Walking with him during this process was not easy. But as more time went by, Don increasingly opened up, placed his faith in God, and became more and more confident.

At the same time, God was chipping away at my pride, my sin, and my lack of dependence upon him. I was amazed at the joy Don displayed despite his circumstances. I was also drawn to his giftedness and his ability to make people around him feel valuable. I was considered his champion, his biggest fan, but he championed me. Our friendship was not a sacrifice in any way; it was a gift meant to remind me of God's goodness and how much I need him. Suddenly, and without really knowing how, I came to realize that my life was richer and deeper with Don in it. I was beginning to thrive.

Before the class was completed, Don got a job at an art supply store, moved into an apartment, and started dating the love of his life.

A few years later, I had the unique opportunity to pray at Don's wedding. He and Sheri, his bride, asked me to be a part of their special day. As Don prepared to give his vows to Sheri, he handed out three scrolls—one to me, one to the pastor, and one to Sheri's father. On the scroll were the vows he had written to her. But before he read them to her, he turned to the congregation and said, "I have given these vows to the men in my life so they can keep me accountable to them."

A man who had been an enemy of God, who did not want to be around people ever again, now was a child of God experiencing the love of family and friends and the dignity of work.

Another man who thought God owed him something recognized his deep need for God and, in circumstances only God can orchestrate, found giving his life to others and learning what it looks like to be just is where real life is found.

Without each other, adrift and languishing. But together? Surprisingly, unexpectedly, gloriously . . . thriving.

QUESTIONS TO CONSIDER

1. Think of a time when you prejudged someone inaccurately based on a first impression. What helped you see there was more to the story?
2. Who are the "Dons" in your story that have changed the way you see the world? What lessons did you learn from them?
3. What are we missing out on when we don't have a "Don" in our lives?

CHAPTER 3

God's Heart for Justice

Before he had reached his twenty-first birthday, Frank Abagnale Jr. was an international con artist who was wanted in over a dozen countries for check forgery and assuming at least eight different false identities. Abagnale claims to have worked as an assistant state attorney general in Louisiana, a hospital physician in Georgia, and a Pan American World Airways pilot.

He assumed the identity of a pilot so he could fly wherever he wanted for free. To do so, he called Pan Am and told them he was a pilot who had lost his uniform. They provided him with a new one. After getting the pilot's uniform, Abagnale forged a Federal Aviation Administration pilot's license and logged over two million air miles!

Abagnale ultimately spent over four years in prison but was then offered a job by the federal government to help them stop con artists such as himself.[2]

Our identity matters. When watching *Catch Me If You Can*, the movie that depicts Frank Abagnale's story starring Leonardo DiCaprio and Tom Hanks, I was fascinated to think about the false identities someone could take on and actually get away with it.

I wonder if you relate to Abagnale at all. Chances are you haven't developed a string of elaborate cons like him. But you may struggle to know your true identity. Does it come from what you've built? From what others think of you? Or from somewhere else entirely?

Here's the answer: Our truest identity doesn't come from what we do;

it comes from God. We take on the identities God gives us that reflect His character and who He is.

As we begin our journey to understand what it means to be a just leader, our first step is to develop a clear picture of the way God feels about justice. We need to realize that justice isn't simply something God *does*. It's something God *is*. It's inherent to his identity.

If justice is central to God's very identity—if it is, as I'm claiming, his very heartbeat—then Christians should be incredibly familiar with the idea. But many of us seem to have overlooked the ways in which God talks about justice in our Bibles. The theme itself runs from cover to cover. We simply haven't taken it in.

If you're a person of faith, this is an unsettling truth. It's uncomfortable to be told that we're ignoring the very identity of the God we claim to follow. Allow that discomfort to convict you, but don't get stuck there. Instead, allow God's Spirit to guide you to know him better. It's not weakness, but wisdom, to admit we need to learn.

And if you *aren't* a person of faith, feel free to continue reading this book (and in particular this chapter) over the shoulders of us Christians. You'll agree with some aspects, and I imagine you'll disagree with others. Regardless, I hope you're encouraged by the principles we uncover and excited to see God's heart for justice.

WHAT IS BIBLICAL JUSTICE?

The primary word for *justice* in the Bible is *mishpat*. It indicates a rectifying justice—making everything as it's supposed to be. When *mishpat* is in effect, people are treated equitably. They are given their rights or their due when they act rightly, and they are punished when acting wrongly.

Mishpat, in many ways, is the type of justice we understand—reward those who do well; punish those who break the rules or do evil.

But it goes even further than that. It's also restorative—providing restoration for those who are victims of injustice. And it's quite interesting to note that "the restorative side of mishpat is far more prominent in Scripture than the retributive side."[3]

We see this as certain people groups are mentioned often with *mishpat*—orphans, widows, foreigners, the poor (referred to as the quartet of the vulnerable). One of the prophets, Zechariah, provides a characteristic mention of this quartet:

*Thus says the Lord of hosts, Render true judgments, show kindness and mercy to one another, do not oppress **the widow, the fatherless, the sojourner, or the poor**, and let none of you devise evil against another in your heart. (Zechariah 7:9–10, emphasis added)*

As Tim Keller noted in *Generous Justice*, the *mishpat* of a society (or its level of justness) is measured by how much it cares for and restores these groups of people.[4] A lack of doing this is a violation of justice.

Whoever oppresses a poor man insults his Maker, but he who is generous to the needy honors him. (Proverbs 14:31)

God is saying our lack of caring for those in need around us is not just a bad idea or insensitive— it's an insult to him. It's like we are thumbing our nose at God, turning our backs and walking the other way.

I don't know about you, but that scares me. I don't want to be seen as someone who thumbs his nose at God.

The other Hebrew word used in Scripture to refer to justice is *tzadeqah* (SAH-dih-KAH). Unlike *mishpat*, which means "rectifying justice," *tzadeqah* means "righteousness" or "primary justice." It's the idea that everything is in right relationship to everything else. We have a right relationship with God, ourselves, others, and creation. All of those relationships are governed by fairness, generosity, and equity.

Brian Fikkert and Steve Corbett write in *When Helping Hurts*:

Being made in the image of God, human beings are inherently relational. Before the fall, God established four foundational relationships for each person—a relationship with God, with self, with others, and with creation. . . . When these relationships are functioning properly, people are able to fulfill their calling of glorifying God by working and supporting themselves and their families with the fruit of that work.[5]

When *tzadeqah* is perfectly present, there is no need for *mishpat*; nothing's broken, so nothing needs to be fixed. Everyone in society is thriving.

Throughout the Old Testament, you will see *mishpat* (usually translated "justice") and *tzadeqah* (usually translated "righteousness") listed together often.

*He loves **righteousness and justice**; the earth is full of the steadfast love of the Lord. (Psalm 33:5, emphasis added)*

***Righteousness and justice** are the foundation of your throne; steadfast love and faithfulness go before you. (Psalm 89:14, emphasis added)*

*"I am the Lord who practices steadfast love, **justice, and righteousness** in the earth. For in these things I delight, declares the Lord." (Jeremiah 9:24b, emphasis added)*

This is God's definition of social justice. *Tzadeqah* is the social part (right relationships), and *mishpat* is the justice part (making everything as it's supposed to be).

Let me pause here for a second, because I know just mentioning the phrase *social justice* is bound to raise some eyebrows.

Much debate has taken place among Christians about the term social justice, and whether it is appropriate to use and even pursue by churches who follow Jesus.[6] Because of the history of the term and the myriad of ways it has been used, it's understandable that people are wary. When someone refers to "social justice," it is not clear exactly what they mean since there are so many interpretations.

I've found Tim Keller's perspective to be very helpful here. In a 2020 article, Pastor Keller contrasted some of the most prominent views of justice operative in our society, showing how none of them measure up to the biblical picture. Keller writes:

Christians know little about biblical justice, despite its prominence in the Scriptures. This ignorance is having two effects. First, large swaths of the church still do not see "doing justice" as part of their calling as individual believers. Second, many younger Christians, recognizing this failure of the church and wanting to rectify things, are taking up one or another of the secular approaches to justice, which introduces distortions into their practice and lives.[7]

Keller's article is worth reading in its entirety. But the relevant point for our discussion is this: The best way out of the maze of secular approaches to social justice is not to ditch social justice; rather, it is to lean into the Bible's "ancient, rich, strong, comprehensive, complex, and attractive understanding of justice."[8]

Not everything under the banner of *justice* is worthy of the name. This is why it's so important to get biblical justice *right*. The pervasiveness of *mishpat* and *tzadeqah* through the pages of Scripture show that justice is important to God—the earth is full of it, it's the foundation of his throne, and he delights in it—and therefore should be important to those who want to follow him.

So what exactly *is* biblical justice? Here are six of the most prominent features:

1. Justice is a part of who God is. It's in his DNA.
For the Lord is a God of justice. (Isaiah 30:18)

Father of the fatherless and protector of widows is God in his holy habitation. (Psalm 68:5)

If you remember nothing else, remember this: Justice is not just what God *does*, it is who he *is*. He is the God of justice. That's his identity. In Psalm 68, he even gives himself names that refer to his justice identity—the Father of the fatherless, the protector of widows. These are like his superhero names.

2. Justice is what he loves.

For I, the LORD, love justice. I hate robbery and wrong. (Isaiah 61:8)

Nothing surprising here, right? If justice is central to who God is in his perfection, then it stands to reason that God *loves* justice. The inverse of this is also true: God hates injustice. Every time we are brokenhearted or enraged at the injustice of our world, we are reflecting God's heart. In fact, he hates injustice even more than we do!

3. Justice is what Jesus came to do.

*"The Spirit of the Lord is on me, because he has anointed me to **proclaim good news to the poor.** He has sent me to **proclaim freedom for the prisoners and recovery of sight for the blind, to set the oppressed free,** to proclaim the year of the Lord's favor. (Luke 4:18-19, NIV, emphasis added)*

Some context: This is Jesus's first sermon. He's setting the tone for his entire ministry here. It's tough to overstate the importance of the text he chooses.

So where does Jesus go? What Bible passage does he use for his stage-setting sermon? In Luke 4, we see that Jesus begins by quoting Isaiah 61:1-2, which is the "I, the Lord, love justice" passage we just mentioned.

In doing this, Jesus indicates not only that this is his mission while on earth, but also that he is the fulfillment of this passage. When he was finished reading, he closed the scroll and said, "Today this Scripture has been fulfilled in your hearing" (Luke 4:21).

Jesus came to earth so that those who believe in him could have a right relationship with God—to be justified before the Creator of the universe. He did that by receiving the just punishment we deserved for our sin and went to the cross to die in our place.

And because he defeated sin and death, he also came to administer justice on earth as it is in heaven—to make everything as it is supposed to be—to proclaim freedom for the prisoners and recovery of sight for the blind, to set the oppressed free, and to proclaim the year of the Lord's favor. To be about *mishpat* and *tzadeqah*. To promote the kingdom in which *all* people truly thrive.

4. Justice is what God commands his people to do.

*And what does the Lord require of you **but to do justice**, and to love kindness, and walk humbly with your God. (Micah 6:8, emphasis added)*

If justice is a core element of who God is, if justice is something God loves, if justice is what Jesus came to do, then it only stands to reason that his followers should do the same. And sure enough, in this passage (as in many others), God makes it plain: Those who follow him are commanded to be people who speak, act, and live with justice.

5. Justice and mercy to those in need are inevitable signs of justifying faith in God.

*But if anyone has the world's goods and sees his brother in need, yet closes his heart against him, **how does God's love abide in him?** (1 John 3:17, emphasis added)*

This verse should make a Christian pause. John compares the extent to which we care for those who are hurting and pursue justice to the level of God's love inside of us. If one is absent, so is the other. In other words, if we don't pursue justice for those in need, people can question whether God's love is even inside of us. Whoa!

If you are a Christian and you want to know whether your faith is real, check to see how much love and care you have for your brother or sister in need.

If you don't like the answer you're getting, don't look away. Turn to God and ask him to make things different. Ask him to make you different.

6. By spending ourselves for those in need, we experience the fullness of God and have our deepest needs met.

> *If you pour yourself out for the hungry and satisfy the desire of the afflicted,*
> *then shall your light rise in the darkness and your gloom be as the noonday.*
> *And the Lord will guide you continually and satisfy your desire in scorched places*
> *and make your bones strong; and you shall be like a watered garden, like a spring*
> *of water, whose waters do not fail. And your ancient ruins shall be rebuilt; you*
> *shall raise up the foundations of many generations; you shall be called the repairer*
> *of the breach, the restorer of streets to dwell in. (Isaiah 58:10-12)*

These verses are very important to understand. The prophet Isaiah is letting God's people know what a true fast is, one that God honors. Basically, a true fast is one in which you truly give yourselves to those who are broken and in need.

That much might not be very surprising. But the results are. Notice that he does not tell them the result is *for those who are broken and in need.* No, the result is for those who spend themselves for those in need, the ones who pursue justice. Read that again with my emphasis added:

> ***Your** light shall rise in the darkness*
> ***Your** gloom will be as the noonday*

*The Lord will guide **you** continually*
*He will satisfy **your** desires*
*He will make **your** bones strong*
***You** shall be like a well watered garden whose waters do not fail*
***Your** ancient ruins shall be rebuilt*
***You** shall raise up the foundations of many generations*
***You** shall be called repairer of the breach, the restorer of streets to dwell in.*
(Isaiah 58:10–12)

I don't know about you, but I would like my life to be characterized by the promises above. And God gives us the formula to experience them: "If you pour yourself out for the hungry and satisfy the desire of the afflicted." In other words, the path to *your* personal thriving and the path of justice don't meet like a fork in the road; they are one path. By pursuing one, you pursue the other.

This is what I experienced, in small part, with Don. And it's what Pastor McCoy and Chris understood when they pursued each other and ultimately started Jobs for Life. They were cultivating justice. But along the way, they learned that *justice* people are also whole people. Justice multiplies the fullness of God—not just in others, but in you.

Justice could not be more central to who God is and what he's about. If you are a follower of Jesus, it should be central to who you are and what you're about.

So, I want to ask you what might be an uncomfortable question: *Do you see yourself as a man or woman of justice?*

How does that sit with you? Do those clothes fit? Can you say, just like God does, "Hi, I'm [insert your name] and I'm a [(man/woman] of justice"?

In fact, can you say the following?

- Justice is a part of who I am. It's in my DNA.
- Justice is what I love.

- Justice is what I am on earth to do.
- Justice is what God commands me to do.
- Justice and mercy to those in need are inevitable signs of my justifying faith in God.
- By spending myself for those in need, I experience the fullness of God and have my deepest needs met.

Here's the bad news: None of us can muster up enough goodness to say those sentences, in good conscience, in our own power.

But here's the good news: If you love Jesus, and have been justified by him, *that's exactly who you are and what he's called you to be*—a man or woman of justice. What your ambition could never achieve, his Spirit can do through you.

Don't believe me? The Bible actually shows us a case study for this kind of transformation. One man, completely unable to (and uninterested in) pursuing justice, meets with Jesus.

And suddenly everything changes.

QUESTIONS TO CONSIDER

1. What did you learn about God's view of justice that you didn't know before?
2. How does God's definition of justice differ from the way the world defines justice?
3. Do you see yourself as a man or woman of justice?
4. How might your life change if you saw yourself as a man or woman of justice?
5. How might your leadership change if you saw yourself as a man or woman of justice?

CHAPTER 4

Everyone Wins

Everyone in his city hated him. And for good reason. He was a traitor and an extortionist. Sure, everyone resented the occupying armies since they oppressed, crushed, and enslaved this small minority group. But what this man did was worse . . . because he was part of that minority. And instead of standing in solidarity with his brothers and sisters, he started working for the corrupt, invading government.

He knew the government officials hated him, too. But if he acted as their muscle, collecting debts from his neighbors, at least he'd have a paycheck.

Apparently, though, his bank account (filled with unjust wealth) wasn't leading to the life of security and fulfillment he had hoped for. So, when he heard about a local religious teacher coming to town, something intrigued him. Something so compelling that, for once, he didn't care how he looked to the people around him. He was going to do everything he could to see this man.

We don't know why, but there must have been something inside of him that was longing for more. Maybe he was tired of being the enemy. Maybe he realized his money and possessions would never satisfy him. Maybe he was lonely, afraid, tired, depressed, and hopeless. But he was not going to miss this chance.

So, what did this hardened, hated, ruthless man do?

He climbed a tree.

If you haven't picked up on it by now, I'm talking about Zacchaeus. He might be remembered in the kids' songs as "a wee little man," but it's hard to imagine anyone who typifies injustice like him. Surely Jesus, the Son of God whose mission was to bring justice into the world, wouldn't seek out a man like Zacchaeus.

So it must have been a complete surprise—not just to the crowd, but to Zacchaeus, too—when Jesus called his name, and his name alone, as he passed by. He wasn't scolding Zacchaeus or pointing out his unjust ways. Instead, he said to him, "Zacchaeus, come down immediately. I must stay at your house today."

So Zacchaeus did. And Jesus did.

What must have been going through Zacchaeus's mind? *Jesus has chosen* me? *Why?* Out of everyone in the crowd, Jesus not only singled Zacchaeus out; he also wanted to spend time with him in his home, the most culturally intimate act in Jewish culture.

Jesus did not require Zacchaeus to clean up his ways or get his act together before choosing him. Moreover, Jesus turned the tables on the way the crowd felt about Zacchaeus. They would have looked up at him in the tree with shame and ridicule. But by getting close to Zacchaeus in this way, Jesus took that shame on himself.

No matter what Zacchaeus had done, Jesus had chosen him. That one fact made all the difference. So from that moment forward, Zacchaeus placed his faith in Jesus.

We know Zacchaeus trusted Jesus because of what he decided to do with his money. He exclaimed, "Look, Lord! Here and now, I give half of my possessions to the poor, and if I have cheated anybody out of anything, I will pay back four times the amount."

Zacchaeus's response was extraordinary. The law required people to give away 10 percent of their money, but he said he would give away half (50 percent) of it. In addition, if you cheated anyone, the law required that you had to pay back what you took with 20 percent interest (see Leviticus 6:2–5), so you had to give 120 percent back. But Zacchaeus said he would pay back four times the amount, or 400 percent.

But the greatest giving hadn't even started yet.

Zacchaeus was giving a lot. But realizing Zacchaeus's faith, Jesus gave him what he desperately needed—salvation.

Jesus said to him, "Today salvation has come to this house, because this man, too, is a son of Abraham. For the Son of Man came to seek and to save the lost" (Luke 19:9–10).

Zacchaeus did nothing to deserve Jesus's justification. He didn't earn his salvation through his generosity. Jesus pointed to the inner transformation that had happened in Zacchaeus's heart that caused him to let go and be generous in the one area he had always allowed to define him: the power and status he got through his money.

One of the worst sinners—a wealthy traitor and extortionist—was not outside of Jesus's reach.

FROM ZACCHAEUS'S TREE TO JESUS'S TREE

It's difficult for me to relate to Zacchaeus. To my knowledge, I have not been a traitor or an extortionist. In fact, I was the opposite. Growing up in a Christian environment, there was never a day I did not know who Jesus was. I wanted to go to church and learn more about God. And I wanted what came with that: safety, affirmation, good friendships, and ultimately, salvation. I made good grades, was athletic, didn't drink, and tried to do the right thing to earn God's favor. I knew I was sinful, but I didn't think I was *that* sinful. Sure, I needed a Savior, but others needed a Savior a lot more than me.

Especially people like Zacchaeus.

It wasn't until later that I realized how my pride and selfishness drove everything I did. Relationships like the one I had with Don helped me to see that my self-reliance and low view of my sin were toxic. That there was nothing I could do to justify myself. That I was far more like Zacchaeus than I cared to admit. Only God's grace and mercy could justify me.

And he has, just like he did for Zacchaeus. He called Zacchaeus down from a shameful tree, and Jesus eventually was crucified, in shame, on a different tree—all to justify those who believe in him. Jesus swapped places with Zacchaeus, taking Zacchaeus's shame and offering him salvation instead. He swapped places with me, taking my sin and shame and offering me God's righteousness. Zacchaeus didn't see the full picture that day, but we Christians, having the full story, do: We know that Jesus bore God's wrath for our sin, paying the just payment our sins demanded and wiping them away once and for all by defeating sin and death when he rose on the third day.

For Christians who believe this, we are justified and therefore should be very familiar with justice. In fact, we should be the first ones in line advocating for justice in light of what Jesus has done for us. Justification is a remarkable gift we do not deserve, and therefore, it should mark the way we live.

Which leads us to the very first foundational marks of being a just leader. Are you ready? You sure?

Just leaders are leaders who rest. Yes, *rest*.

Let that sink in. For real. Take a moment . . .

We leaders are people who typically run a thousand miles an hour. We're churning; we're grinding. For some of us, that's the way we're wired, which has led us to the success we have achieved. For others of us, we feel we have no choice. Resting is a sign of weakness, laziness.

But consider this: If your faith is in Jesus and you have been completely justified by what He has done for you, the worst-case scenario for your future is unending bliss in a perfect world where everything works as it is supposed to. You will have a perfect body and live forever in a world marked by overflowing joy, deep love, authentic community, glorifying work, complete wholeness, wonderful light, and eternal worship.

Pretty awesome, right?

JUST LEADERS ARE LEADERS WHO REST

With that as your destiny, you can be a leader who is at rest in the present. Thriving as a leader and being just can never flow from a restless heart. So, if you are not at rest, you cannot begin to be the just leader God is calling you to be.

Being at rest is the foundation of a just leader.

That doesn't mean we go slower than we should in fighting against injustice and brokenness. When God says, "Learn to do good; seek justice, correct oppression" (Isaiah 1:17), it's clear we are called to take up the cause of the vulnerable and marginalized with urgency.

But if that work is going to be effective and sustainable, it has to come from a place of deep soul rest. Our circumstances will not always feel restful. Often it will be the opposite. But our spirits will be at rest, which will give us the courage and fortitude to persevere through the storm. A spirit of rest will anchor us as we fight the winds of injustice.

So, let me ask some questions as we begin to think about what it means to be a just leader:

- How are you resting? Is your soul at rest? Do you know Jesus as your Savior, and do you rest in him?
- How are you sleeping? Are you anxious, exhausted, uptight, nervous?
- What is making you stressed? Are you worried about money? Your business? The people you lead? Your spouse? Your children? Your reputation? Your career? Your friendships?
- In short, what is keeping you up at night?

I can't imagine Zacchaeus being a restful soul prior to meeting Jesus. He wasn't thriving. He was hustling. When you're constantly scheming about getting ahead, there simply isn't time to stop. Not to mention his heart, which was diametrically opposed to the just heart of God. A life of extortion is also a life of restlessness.

In contrast, just leaders are at peace, which leads to a life of rest.

I had to learn this the hard way. For a solid year, I couldn't sleep. On Sunday evenings, I could feel myself getting anxious anticipating what was ahead for me on Monday morning. I would enter the week having rested over the weekend, but by the time Wednesday or Thursday would roll around, I would be waking up each morning at 3:00 or 3:30 a.m. without being able to go back to sleep.

My mind would be racing with all the cares and concerns of work. By the end of the week, I was a zombie.

Recognizing the impact this was having on me, our board chair took me aside one day and said, "David, we [the board] are giving you a sabbatical. You *have* to rest. You need to change, the organization needs to change, and there is no way that can happen if you don't completely separate and get away."

I was shocked. I didn't realize it had gotten that bad. They were telling me to leave, check out, take a break. On the one hand I was ecstatic. A three-month vacation! Somebody pinch me!

On the other hand, I felt like I had failed. I couldn't handle it. Certainly a tougher person could have held up under this pressure. Now they were saying they didn't *need* me? How would everything get done?

Well, believe it or not, it did. Everything I had worried about somehow got done. Our team stepped up, took on more responsibility, and I got a much-needed break.

In the process, I learned to chill out, to truly believe that God is in control of my work, not me. His promises are certain, and I don't need to worry. That put me on a path of building in rhythms of rest I never would have pursued without the opportunity to step back.

Just leaders are leaders who work *out of their rest* rather than just *rest from their* work.

What does that mean?

They recognize that God is in control of every aspect of their lives, especially their work. Whether they eat or drink, or whatever they do, they do it all for the glory of God (see 1 Cor 10:31). They have a proper view of themselves and their work, and they don't believe they are indispensable. Therefore, they are content, free, and calm, and *even when times are rough*, they trust God's promises and are confident in the security he offers.

They trust the people they lead, and they think more about investing in others than in themselves. They have a long view and demonstrate unwavering patience rather than being consumed by the tyranny of the urgent.

For some, it's practically impossible to view leadership from a place of rest. The workplace, particularly in the United States, prides itself on busyness and seems to prey on people and companies who don't keep their nose to the grindstone. Rise and grind. Hustle. Stay hungry.

But here's the thing: *God* rested, and he set a pattern of rest for us—not as an obligation but as a gift.

The biblical idea of Sabbath—resting from our work—is the first day of the week, not the last.[9] We work, therefore, out of the reality that we are OK, our future is secure, and we do not have to work ourselves to the bone both physically and emotionally only to collapse at the end of the week. It's the idea of putting rest first.

When we think about being a just leader, we immediately rush to the idea of what we need to fix or what injustice we need to solve. For many of us, that's just in the way we're made. It's in our DNA.

Resting? Not so much.

Understanding that Jesus has justified us so we are secure rarely crosses our mind. But it's the foundation for justice. It's why Zacchaeus was so radically generous with his money—the thing that had given him power and identity. He was willing to let it go in astounding amounts because he knew he didn't need it anymore. It did not provide what he was looking for.

Only Jesus did.

JUST LEADERS ARE LEADERS WHO DREAM

Once we know we're at rest, we then can be leaders who *dream*.

No longer are we motivated by guilt and shame, no matter what we have. We can use our creativity and imagination to steward what God has given us to be a just leader and pursue biblical justice.

Dreaming is the fuel that drives a just leader.

I want to give you a picture of what this looks like through a small yet powerful verse found in Proverbs.

When the righteous prosper, the city rejoices. (Proverbs 11:10, NIV)

Only seven words (four in Hebrew!), but their meaning cannot be overstated.

First, *the righteous*. Who are they? The word for *righteous* is the Hebrew word *tsaddiqim* (Sah-dih-KEEM). It is used more than two hundred times in the Old Testament to refer to people who are considered to embody righteousness. (We saw a version of this word in the previous chapter—*tsaddeqah*, which means "righteousness.")

This word, *tsaddiqim*, doesn't just mean piety or doing what's right. It's much deeper than that.

Dr. Amy Sherman, in her book *Kingdom Calling*, describes the *tsaddiqim* as:

the just—people in love with God and His Kingdom . . .
who see their prosperity as a blessing to be used not just for themselves, but for others. . .
and therefore steward everything they have (when I say everything I mean everything—their power, gifts, position, influence, money, time, education, relationships, networks, home, etc.) to pursue God's peace (*shalom*, which means complete wholeness) and justice (*mishpat*, everything is as it's supposed to be).[10]

In other words, the *tsaddiqim* don't steward what they have out of guilt and shame. Instead, they use their creative imagination and faith, knowing everything they have comes from God. Freed from the tyranny of their own selfishness, they become people who can *dream* of justice.

Perhaps they are on the margins of society, and they use that unique position to highlight injustice and paint a picture of true wholeness. After all, it historically has been victims of injustice and oppression who have been able to see themselves most clearly in the gospel message and view Jesus for who he really is.

Or perhaps they are those at the top of society, who instead of being captivated by power and prestige, disadvantage themselves for the advantage of others and find life where they least expect it.

Regardless of their position, the *tsaddiqim* have cultivated eyes to see what few others see, hearts to care for what God cares for—justice. And they put their hands to work transforming dreams of justice into reality.

This goes way beyond the notion of "giving back" or the traditional idea of charity, where we give to those in need out of our excess. This is whole life stewardship of all we have to create fairness, generosity, and equity.

Second, the word *rejoices*. It's *taalos*. In other places in Scripture, this word gets translated as "exult" or "triumph."

This isn't just joy but *jumping* for joy. Think of a wild, unbridled, exuberant celebration—people dancing in the streets.

- This is V-E Day on May 8, 1945, when millions of people across the world ran into the streets for a wild celebration when Germany surrendered to mark the end of World War II.

- This is June 19, 1865, when more than 250,000 slaves in Texas wildly celebrated all across the state when Union soldiers showed up in Galveston to let them know they were free (even though they *had* been freed legally two years before through the Emancipation Proclamation). This day is Juneteenth, now a federal holiday, and is commemorated as the actual day slavery ended in the United States.

- This is April 5, 1993, when I, along with my best friends, ran as fast as we could to dance on Franklin Street in Chapel Hill, North Carolina, with thousands of our fellow classmates after the North Carolina Tar Heels won the national championship in basketball against the Michigan Wolverines.

You get the picture. The word *rejoices* is describing an absolute party. People are beside themselves with joy. There even is a war connotation with this word—meaning the war is over, our oppressors are gone, and we have won!

Third, when it says *the city*, it refers to *the whole city*, people at the very top and people at the very bottom—meaning that even the poorest of the poor or those who are most marginalized are dancing in the streets.

So, why is the whole city rejoicing?

The answer here is a startling one: The city is rejoicing **because the righteous are prospering**. Things are going well with them. They are gaining more power, wealth, and influence. They are thriving like never before. And as a result, *everyone* is thrilled.

Now, let's stop and think about this. Does this make sense? People getting richer? People gaining more power? We can understand that. It happens all the time. But instead of rejoicing, wouldn't that make others resentful and discouraged, bitter and angry?

Not this time.

Why?

Because they know that when the *tsaddiqim* win, everyone wins. The *tsaddiqim* thrive in ways that multiply.

Everyone winning can be a difficult concept to grasp. We hardly have a grid for it in our world of winners and losers. That was the hope with trickle-down economics, but in order for trickle-down economics to work, you have to have people at the top willing to sacrifice for the whole. Otherwise, the rich get richer, the poor get poorer, and there is no change in the power dynamic.

But that's not what we see in Proverbs 11:10. Apparently, when *these* people (the righteous) win, it actually makes life better for everyone, even those on the margins. A fractured community, somehow, turns into a flourishing one.

The *tsaddiqim* use all of who they are and what they have been given not for themselves but for the pursuit of God's peace and justice. And when they do that, the city rejoices.

A city Dr. Sherman says that is marked with:[11]

- Beauty
- Unity
- Security
- Lack of violence
- Wholeness
- Hope
- Comfort
- Economic flourishing
- Sustainability
- Peace with God

With all that's going on in the world, don't we want that?

Does that sound like a dream to you? A bit of far-fetched optimism? It may not be the world most of us live in every day, but I believe it's possible.

The question for us—the very point of this book—is: *How can we be like the* tsaddiqim— *leaders who are just?* No matter how much we have, all of us have a measure of power, wealth, and influence. How might God use each one of us to make our whole city rejoice?

We have a choice: Either we use that power, wealth, and influence to build our own kingdoms (ending up like Zacchaeus, restless and stuck in the nightmare of our own creation), or we use our power, wealth, and influence to build businesses, organizations, and cities of peace and justice.

The prophet Jeremiah once wrote, "Seek the peace and prosperity of the city to which I have carried you into exile. Pray to the Lord for it, because if it prospers, you too will prosper" (Jeremiah 29:7, NIV). When we seek the prosperity of others, we prosper, too. Leaders thrive by being just.

We can thrive. We can rest. And we can *dream* about the future God is building in our midst. We can be people with a vision for justice and steward all we have so the whole city can rejoice. I know—because I've seen it happen.

So . . . how can we become leaders like this? I want to give you four qualities of a *just leader* based on what we see from the ultimate *tsaddiqim*, Jesus, and the ways he pursued justice:

- *Just leaders* see the whole playing field.
- *Just leaders* build cultural competency.
- *Just leaders* give power away.
- *Just leaders* take bold, courageous action.

You ready? Let's do this!

QUESTIONS TO CONSIDER

1. What aspects of Zacchaeus's story challenge you the most?
2. What are you holding on to for security that you need to let go of (money, success, relationships, peace, safety, accomplishment, etc.)?
3. How can you begin to work out *of* your rest rather than just rest *from* your work?
4. Do you see yourself as the *tsaddiqim*? Why or why not? How might your understanding of the *tsaddiqim* provide a vision for your life and leadership?
5. What would your success need to look like for your city to rejoice?

See the Whole Playing Field

I grew up playing basketball. Every afternoon after school, I would go out to the driveway behind our house where we had set up a hoop, and I would shoot for hours. Friends would come over, and we'd have epic battles. We would lower the goal to seven or eight feet and play Dunkball, which essentially is normal basketball, but with the lowered goal, we could slam it in someone's face or go up for an alley-oop dunk! I'd wear a sweatband on my left forearm just like Michael Jordan did early in his career, and I'd act like I could levitate just like him.

But Michael Jordan I was not. Little did I know, my body was only three or four inches off the ground when I went up for the slam.

Most kids learning to play basketball gravitate to games like Dunkball, trying high-flying dunks or making crazy moves at the basket. Unfortunately, most coaches don't. Early on, they don't even want kids focusing on shooting and scoring.

Instead, coaches want players simply to learn how to dribble the ball. Why? For two main reasons: 1) Dribbling is the main way you get around the court. It's Basketball 101; and 2) You need to see the whole court, and you can't see anything if you're staring down at the ball.

I've heard coaches yell a thousand times, "Keep your head up!" Dribbling needs to be automatic, because in basketball, vision is everything.

When you have the ball, you not only need to see what you have to do, but you have to know what every player on your team is doing. And you need to anticipate and see what the opposition is going to do. None of which you can do with your eyes closed.

When we are confronted with injustice, the natural question we ask is, "What do we need to *do*?" But that's a bit like starting with Dunkball. It's an enticing entry point, but it's not the most helpful. "What do we *do*?" isn't the first question we should ask ourselves. Instead, like a point guard, we should ask, "What do we need to *see*?"

As Daniel Hill writes in *White Awake*:

> It is particularly important for White Americans to approach this subject matter with the right goals in mind. Our goal must be sight. Our goal must be transformation. Our goal must be a renewed consciousness.[12]

Jesus was a master at seeing. When he looked at others, he did not just see them—he knew them.

> *Seeing the people, **he felt compassion for them, because they were distressed and dispirited like sheep without a shepherd.** (Matthew 9:36, NASB, emphasis added)*

Seeing takes work. It takes intentionality. It takes patience. Just leaders don't just live in their own world, they have their heads up and can see things around them others can't see.

They see themselves, others, and their community.

CHAPTER 5

What We Need to See in Ourselves

One of the first steps to being just is to be keenly self-aware—to have emotional intelligence about ourselves. To know what we're good at, what we're not good at, what motivates us, what makes us anxious, what we hope for, and how we relate to others.

In 1955, psychologists Joseph Luft and Harry Ingham developed the Johari Window as a model for self-awareness and a way for leaders to enhance understanding and communication with those they lead.[13] The name *Johari* is a combination of their two names, Joe and Harry. Love it!

The Johari Window model is used to enhance an individual's perception of others. It is based on two ideas: Trust can be acquired by 1) revealing information about yourself to others and 2) also learning about yourself from their feedback.

This is the Johari Window:

	KNOWN TO SELF	NOT KNOWN TO SELF
KNOWN TO OTHERS	OPEN	BLIND SPOT
NOT KNOWN TO OTHERS	HIDDEN/FACADE	UNKNOWN

Two of the panes represent what is known and unknown to ourselves. The other two panes represent what is known and unknown to others. People intersect with each pane based on the ways they interact with and receive feedback from others.

1. Open—In this pane, information about yourself and your thoughts, feelings, skills, views, and behavior are known by you and by others. These actions and thoughts are readily shared and demonstrated by you and therefore easily perceived and understood by people around you. For instance, I'm six feet tall and grew up in Nashville, Tennessee. I eat Wheaties or Cheerios every morning and usually have chocolate chip cookie dough on tap so I can make two warm cookies for dessert most nights. I love sports and would rather watch a game at night than go to a party where I do not know anyone. I know these things about myself— and anyone who knows me knows these things about me, too.

2. Blind spot—This is information about yourself that others know about you, but you don't—aspects of yourself revealed in the actions, the way you look, or the reactions you have that everyone can see except you. For instance, I often get food stuck in my teeth. Unfortunately, this is a blind spot of mine. On more occasions I can count, I will come out of a meeting, get in my car, look in the mirror, and—*oh no!*—I have a black piece of food lodged between my front teeth. (And of course, no one said anything!)

That's a silly example, but blind spots can be much more significant. They can include our unconscious biases—the ways we judge others that are revealed in our posture with them or by what we say that we don't even realize. Or they can be our shortcomings we do not want to admit. We think we are pretty good at something, when everyone else knows we're really not. We're then surprised by the ways people interact with us because *we don't see what we cannot or choose not to see.* Watch a few auditions on *American Idol,* and you'll see what I mean. Some people think they'll win the whole competition when they can't even sing in tune.

It's not always the case, but hearing about our blind spots can be extremely difficult. It therefore is easy to get defensive when they are revealed. A strong leader not only wants to learn about them but also is intentional about asking for feedback from those he or she leads to overcome his or her blind spots.

3. Hidden/façade—This is information you know about yourself, but others don't. You haven't revealed it to them, either because you feel it is private or you are not comfortable enough to let people know. These often are your secrets—feelings, past experiences, or fears. Often, people can feel you are holding back and not trusting them when you hold on to your façades.

I find this to be a significant struggle for leaders. Many leaders believe they need to convey an image of confidence, competence, and authority—to have it all together. These leaders see vulnerability as a weakness, and they think that to show weakness as a leader undermines their leadership.

What these leaders need to recognize is that vulnerability, when rightly exercised, is actually a strength. As social worker and professor Brené Brown puts it, "Vulnerability is not weakness; it's our greatest measure of courage."[14]

People desire social connection, and the best way to achieve that is by getting rid of our façades and embracing vulnerability. The best leaders know how to authentically connect with those they lead by taking risks, opening up about their challenges and fears, and asking for help.

Now, this doesn't mean leaders air *all* of their secrets, *all* of the time. Certainly, there are many occasions where a measure of discretion and hiddenness is not only appropriate but required. But if we think of vulnerability as a spectrum, I've interacted with very few leaders who need the nudge toward *less* vulnerability and *more* discretion. Almost always, the leaders I work with need to be pushed more on the side of being open.

4. Unknown—This is the information which is unknown to yourself and others. Either nothing has happened for you to develop this awareness or you have had experiences, often traumatic, that you suppress and can't recall. It's difficult to discover what may be in this pane, but over time, more may be revealed.

When I was in elementary school, one St. Patrick's Day, I put on a green shirt to go to school. Rarely did I wear green, but the tradition (at least when I was a kid) was that those not wearing green got pinched. I didn't want to get pinched, so green it was. Imagine my surprise, then, when I got pinched all day by my friends.

I was incredulous. I'd say to them, "Why are you pinching me? I'm wearing a green shirt!" And they would respond, "Your shirt isn't green, it's *blue*!"

I should have realized it then, but it wasn't until after college that I discovered I'm color-blind. My color blindness was in the Unknown box when I was in elementary school—I didn't know it; others didn't know it. But now it's in the Open box since I know I'm color-blind, and those who know me know it, too.

Thankfully, I don't get pinched quite as often anymore.

A DIFFERENT KIND OF WINDOW

Let's look at the Johari Window again, this time taking into account what we've just covered.

Over time, the goal for leaders is to minimize the Blind Spot, Unknown, and Hidden/Façade panes so that the Open pane is dominant. Leaders therefore need to ask for feedback, be open to criticism, and check their defensiveness for those areas in their lives they cannot see.

They need to be willing to be vulnerable and reveal areas of their lives they may not feel comfortable sharing. More often than not, leaders need to be careful not to act like they have everything together and instead push themselves to engage authentically and openly with those they lead.

If they do, the Johari Window can begin to look like this:

KNOWN TO SELF   NOT KNOWN TO SELF

KNOWN TO OTHERS

OPEN

NOT KNOWN TO OTHERS

Let's unpack this a bit more. What do we need to see in ourselves to increase our Open pane? We could mention a lot, but here are the five most pressing needs:

1. Our Need for God. I mentioned earlier that I do not remember a day in my life when I did not know who Jesus is and what he has done for me. When I was ten, I went to a Billy Graham Crusade in the Vanderbilt football stadium and decided to go down on the field during the "altar call." Part of me wanted to run on the turf. But more significantly, I truly wanted to trust God and follow Jesus as my Savior.

That led me on a path to try to understand and know God more, read the Bible, learn from others, and be active at our church. "Goody Two Shoes" was a common description I heard from others—a phrase describing someone who was perceived to be uncommonly good. I looked like Opie from *The Andy Griffith Show*, with long, scraggly red hair and knee patches on my Wrangler jeans.

Even though I was fervent in pursuing God, I felt like I had to do all the right things in order to receive his love and acceptance. I truly did not understand the depth of my sin and need for a Savior. And I'm still learning. There is such freedom that comes from his grace, from the desire to move toward him, from the simple choice to walk in righteousness *because of what he has done for me.*

Brennan Manning captured it well in his book, *Ragamuffin Gospel*: "My deepest awareness of myself is that I am deeply loved by Jesus Christ and I have done nothing to earn it or deserve it."[15] At the root, I need God. That's tough for me to say. But liberating, too.

Just leaders know that "there, but for the grace of God, go I." They have a deep dependency upon him and begin to move away from being the center of their universe. They focus their attention on loving God and loving others, knowing that everything they have and everything they are comes from God.

2. Our Unique Value and Giftedness. When I was at Jobs for Life, I absolutely loved watching what would happen in the very first JfL class. Throughout the country, JfL classes are held typically over eight weeks to teach people a biblical understanding of work and help them find and keep meaningful employment. Many of the classes (though not all) are designed for people who have tremendous barriers to work—those coming out of poverty, men and women just released from prison, and individuals wanting to overcome their dependency on government assistance.

In the first class, JfL students learn they are fearfully and wonderfully made, God has designed them with a purpose, and he has a plan for their lives to give them hope and a future. And they learn God created them to work. Work is a part of our DNA; it's the way we are made. The very first thing God did when he created Adam and Eve was to give them a J-O-B: "Fill the earth and subdue it. Rule over the fish of the sea and the birds in the sky, and over every living creature that moves on the ground" (Genesis 1:28, NIV).

You cannot imagine what hearing those truths does to the students in the classes—many of whom have been beaten up by life and have tremendous emotional and even physical scars—to help them understand their unique value and dignity.

One student in particular, Dwight, had grown up in a world of violence. That's all he'd ever known. On his tenth birthday, his estranged father showed up out of the blue, ended up getting in an argument with Dwight's aunt and uncle, and shot them both right in front of Dwight. Later, Dwight ended up in prison for murder (because that's what had been modeled to him). Having been sentenced to life, he miraculously was released after twenty-eight years.

When he walked into the JfL class for the first time, Dwight was, by his own admission, angry at the world. But by the end, that anger had transformed into love and forgiveness. How? he learned he had a purpose. There were people telling him how much God valued and loved him. As he told me later, "I'm able to forgive and not harbor things against people—just release it and let it go. Now I just want to love; I want to help."

Dwight's story is beautifully unique, but I could multiply the basic elements of that story a hundred times over. Because of JfL, many men and women learned for the first time just how deeply they mattered to God—and therefore, how much they could matter to themselves. They learned that work was not a curse, but something they were made to do—continuing God's creation and ultimately worshiping him.

Over the course of the class, they build their vocational plans and uncover their strengths and assets to give fuel and direction to their dreams. Many have never been able to think beyond surviving a single day, or even an hour, so to get to the point where they can consider what their lives could look like over a number of years is a whole new experience. But because they now know they are extraordinary—that God rejoices over them with singing (see Zephaniah 3:16)—they can dream again.

We are often our own worst critics. We compare ourselves to others and wish we were better, could do more, or have more. Comparison is the thief of joy.

God has specifically designed you with a purpose. He loves you and has a plan for you. Just leaders know their value and giftedness. They know what they're good at and don't fret over what they do not have or cannot do that well. They know everything they have is from God, and they do all of their work for his glory.

3. Our Need for Others. Most leaders are lonely. Half of CEOs report experiencing feelings of loneliness in their role, and of this group, 61 percent believe it hinders their performance. First-time CEOs are particularly susceptible to this isolation. Nearly 70 percent of first-time CEOs who experience loneliness report that the feelings negatively affect their performance.[16]

Leaders are misunderstood, often seen as intimidating, and usually have to carry the weight of knowing information they can't share with others. It leads them to be isolated and without authentic relationships.

Jesus said the two greatest commandments are 1) to love God and 2) to love our neighbor. We are made to be in relationship with one another.

High-level leaders can find it extremely difficult to build relationships with peers they can trust.

In my own life, I'm most susceptible to sin, distraction, and unproductivity when I am bored and alone. I mistakenly think I can do whatever I want and not be affected by the consequences.

When this was an acute struggle for me, I called my pastor, Geoff, who is also one of my best friends, and asked if he would be willing for the two of us to go running together every Monday morning. I needed to start off my week with the accountability and support of our friendship. I knew I could not handle what was on my plate as a husband, dad, and leader of an organization without the covering of a regular, committed, mutual friendship.

That was eleven years ago. We now walk instead of run—an inevitable result of getting older—but we have rarely missed a week. We talk, pray, confess sin, share our struggles, and celebrate our joys. It's amazing to see the history of what God has done through our time together as he has answered prayers and sustained us in times of real trial.

Just leaders build authentic relationships with others in which they are completely known. They regularly confess sin in those relationships and refrain from drifting into isolation. Relationships like these are not a given. They require time and a willingness to take a risk. But it's more than worth it.

4. Our History. The desire and means to find out our family histories has grown exponentially in the last twenty-five years. Ancestry.com is one of the significant contributors to that growth. Launched in 1996 as a family history website, Ancestry.com has more than three million paying customers in about thirty countries and earns more than $1 billion in annual revenue.[17]

I'm always amazed when I read genealogies in Scripture. The first chapter of Matthew is a good example. Matthew lists forty-two generations, starting with Abraham and ending with Jesus. That's around one thousand years of records. How did they do that with no Ancestry.com or the ability to check DNA records? I can hardly tell you who my great-grandparents are, let alone my great-great-great-great . . . well, you get the idea.

For many in the United States, family history seems interesting but not absolutely vital. In Scripture, however, family history is huge. Two of the four Gospels list Jesus's genealogy, not because the Gospel writers were trying to fill space, but because genealogies mattered. All throughout the Bible, people are referred to by their family relationships, their heritage. Joshua, son of Nun. David, son of Jesse (and great-grandson of Ruth), from the tribe of Judah. Simon, son of John. Paul, from the tribe of Benjamin. Even God, especially in the Old Testament, is referred to as "the God of our fathers" or "the God of Abraham, Isaac, and Jacob."

For the biblical writers, a person's identity was captured in their history and the family they were a part of. That belief isn't as prevalent in the twenty-first century Western world today. In fact, most of us don't want to be defined by our history. Some of us may not even know our family history. Others, especially Black Americans, may not even have the *option* of knowing their family history, erased as it was by past injustices. But we Americans are the historical oddballs here. What the Bible depicts and many other societies reflect is a fundamental truth: Our history matters, whether we realize it or not. It's much better to know *how it matters* than to let it affect our lives unwittingly.

Some of us have what we have today because of past injustice. That's a tough pill to swallow.

As an example, my grandfather benefited from the GI Bill of 1944. He was able to buy a house as a result of accessing a loan through that program designed for those who served in World War II. Technically, the GI Bill was available to all veterans no matter their race, but it was structured and implemented in such a way that nearly all African American veterans who applied—a staggering *1.2 million*—were denied access to those loans.[18]

As a result, many White families were able to build generational wealth through homeownership not available for most Black families. This injustice has played a significant role in Black families having only one-eighth the wealth of White families today.[19]

My family benefited from the unequal application of the GI Bill. I didn't know that until a few years ago when I was well into my forties. What do I do with that?

Do I feel guilty? Yes.

At fault? Well, no. I wasn't there and had no part in it.

Responsible? Good question. It's something we will touch on later in the book (in chapter 18, "Action That's Disruptive").

Just leaders take steps to know their history. They do so not to be *defined* by it, but to *learn* from it. The more they know their history, the better they understand why they do what they do, why they have what they have, and how they can steward their resources well.

5. Our Unconscious Biases. Unconscious biases are social stereotypes about individuals or certain groups of people that a person develops and doesn't realize. Everyone has unconscious bias; none of us is immune.

We also have *conscious* bias, too, which is a stereotype we *are* aware of. Typically, though, unconscious bias is much more prevalent.

There are several different types of unconscious bias. Here are some examples:

- Gender bias: the tendency to prefer one gender over another gender.
- Name bias: the tendency people have to judge and prefer people with certain types of names—typically names that are of Anglo origin.
- Affinity bias: the tendency people have to connect with others who share similar interests, experiences and backgrounds.
- Beauty bias: social behavior where people believe that attractive people are more successful, competent, and qualified.
- Height bias: the tendency to negatively judge a person who is significantly shorter or taller than the socially accepted human height.[20]

As leaders, our unconscious biases are real blind spots. We have developed them over time, and they impact almost every decision we make. As the above examples demonstrate, they are centered on comparison and preference—ways we unconsciously devalue people or groups in our minds.

It can be difficult to identify your unconscious bias. After all, none of us wants to be biased toward others. We *want* to be people who treat others fairly. But what we say and how we live often don't align.

Harvard University administers an anonymous Implicit Association Tests (IAT) designed to enhance awareness of one's unconscious bias. The test presents various pictures on a computer screen, asks the test taker to respond to the images with either positive or negative descriptive words, and measures the individual's reaction time to determine the strength of the bias. (It's still there and open to the public, by the way. If you're curious, take a few minutes and check it out.[21])

I recently took one of these tests to evaluate my bias toward Black people versus White people. At the end, the results showed the strength of my bias toward one or the other.

I took the test twice. In one test, I had a slight preference for Black people, and in the other, I had a slight preference for White people. Tests like this have limitations, so the results often don't tell the whole story.

Leaders who took the test with me were upset with their results. Some felt they were not accurate, while others felt exposed and didn't know what to do with the results. They were filled with feelings of guilt and shame. All of this is uncomfortable, which is why we avoid it. But it's also very *necessary*.

Just leaders welcome knowing where they have unconscious bias. They are not afraid to have that revealed, nor are they defensive. They understand we all have biases; the question is not *whether* we have them but *how* we discover them.

Go back to the Johari Window: Either we know the biases we are carrying around (making them part of the Open pane) or we *don't* know those biases (making them a Blind Spot). Before we can do anything to change our biases, we've got to see them clearly. None of us will thrive with our heads in the sand.

At this point, though, we're beginning to lift our gaze a bit higher than ourselves. We're starting to look at the people around us. That's a good thing.

This leads us to our next chapter: What do just leaders see in others?

QUESTIONS TO CONSIDER

1. What are three main events in your life that define who you are?
2. Who do you need to ask to help you see your blind spots?
3. What facades are you carrying and with whom do you need to share them?
4. How can you continue to learn about yourself?

CHAPTER 6

What We Need to See in Others

We needed to add to our staff at Jobs for Life. We were looking for someone who could support our work in the field and oversee a number of administrative and customer service tasks. Several candidates applied, but two really stood out.

To determine the right fit, we administered a test to assess the final two candidates' computer and administrative skills. After the test, it was clear that one of the candidates scored higher than the other. We were nearly ready to make an offer. But first we had to run background checks.

At Jobs for Life, we teach those going through the JfL class that they need to be up front with a potential employer if they have something in their background that may be a concern. It's better for them to address it first before the employer does. As one learns in classic sales training, the first one to voice the objection wins.

Unfortunately, there was a serious red flag in the background of the one who scored higher on the computer test. Her report showed "child abuse." I was both surprised and disappointed.

This candidate had not only been impressive but extremely engaging. When asked in the interview why she was interested in the position, she said, "Jobs for Life needs to be a household name!" I loved it. She not only believed that but was ready to make it happen by joining our team.

But she hadn't been candid with us. I was torn. Honestly, I wasn't sure if I could trust her. And this position required a great deal of trust. Plus, child abuse was a serious problem. That was something I could not simply overlook.

Many employers would have moved on from a candidate like her. The issues in her past would have been too much. But something in me kept me from moving on. I wanted to try something different.

So I called her and said, "Shay, we are very interested in you as a candidate for this position, but we found some things in your background that I'm concerned about. Normally, this would be too much to move forward with you, but I want to give you a chance to speak to this before I make a final decision. Is this a good time to talk?"

Shay had never received a call like this from a potential employer. At first, she was taken aback, but then she was completely relieved, even excited, to be given the opportunity to share what was contained in her record.

She distilled a long, detailed story into a ten to fifteen-minute description that was heartbreaking. Shay had been wrongly accused of being "unfit to be a mom" to her son and daughter when they were five and eight years old. She was a single mom at the time, doing everything she could to make a good life for them, but at every turn, people had it out for her.

Living in poverty, she had very few resources and connections to overcome the accusations she faced. Rather than engaging in a long legal battle, she was advised by her court-appointed attorney to give up her parental rights. The alternative was prison, so she took the deal, making the devastating decision to give up her rights. Her children were taken from her and placed in separate foster homes, where Shay had no contact or knowledge of where they were.

It's difficult for me to describe what happened as she recounted her story on that call. We had this honest, real conversation allowing me to enter into her story and understand some of the pain and challenges she had to overcome in her life. Candidly, I struggled to know whether her story was entirely true or not. I hardly knew her and had no way of verifying her story.

But the way she told it deeply impacted me. It was clear she was not telling me this story in order to get the job. (She had already concluded she was out of the running.) Something more significant was going on. People had not given her the opportunity to tell her story. She had never felt validated. And my simple act of giving her the opportunity to explain her background empowered her.

I told Shay at the end of our conversation that I would call her by 3:00 p.m. the next day to let her know my decision.

When I hung up, though, I knew I would hire her for the job.

What wasn't I seeing in Shay at the beginning? What did I see by the end? More importantly, what should just leaders see in others?

As they look at the people around them, just leaders see at least five things:

1. Their History: My phone call with Shay gave me the opportunity to hear her story. That was the beginning of knowing and understanding much more of her background. What I didn't realize was the impact that would have on her. As a Black woman who had been mistreated by White men much of her life, she did not trust White men in authority—you know, someone like me. My simple act of taking the time to understand more fully her background and give her the opportunity to speak openly about her brokenness without judgment changed her perception of me. She started to see me not as a threat but as someone who was genuinely interested in her. I made her feel known, valued, and seen. And as a result, our relationship began on a foundation of trust.

Later, as we worked together and Shay grew into her role, used her gifts, and excelled, she often shared with me how much I had changed her life. She'd do so by displaying immense emotion and tears as she described how I had helped her overcome poverty—not just her physical poverty but her mental and emotional poverty as well.

I don't say this to pat myself on the back. In fact, as she would be speaking with me, I would often think to myself, *Did I miss something? What did I do? Why is she this moved? Wouldn't anyone have done what I did?*

And yet the simple step to know her and understand her totally turned her world upside down. I had no idea.

It's easy for us to miss learning people's stories. It requires intentionality, patience, and a willingness to be vulnerable by genuinely being interested in others. It takes time, which none of us seems to have an excess of. Sometimes, we think people's stories are irrelevant to what we're trying to do or accomplish. That could not be further from the truth.

As leaders, we cannot see people in a vacuum and keep from recognizing the context in which they view and approach life—all of which is informed by their family upbringing, experiences they've had, and their education, relationships, successes, and failures. Admittedly, it can be tricky, particularly in the workplace, to create an environment of trust where people share authentically about who they are and the experiences they have had. People often are hesitant to be open because they do not want the information they share to be used against them, causing them to feel judged, have conflict, not get opportunities to grow, or potentially lose their job. So most people remain distant at work, keep their heads down, do their job, and go home.

But leaders can effectively create a context for people to be truly seen and heard without the threat of negative consequences. It starts by being open themselves (remember the Johari Window?) and then being intentional to take the time to listen to someone's story.

While my conversation with Shay helped me begin to build trust with her, that trust did not happen overnight. When she came to work for me, there were several instances when she struggled to trust me—and vice versa. I didn't understand why something simple I said or did would undermine her trust. On the flip side, there were many days when I was confused by the ways she was feeling or acting, which made me wonder if I could trust her.

And yet, knowing her story allowed me to be patient, resist getting defensive, and give value to her viewpoint. In other circumstances, I would have gotten frustrated, felt like she wasn't the right fit, and never would have hired her in the first place.

2. Their Value and Worth: What do you do when someone on the street asks you for money? Be honest: It's one of the most challenging, frustrating, and awkward situations we face.

Personally, I'm usually pretty conflicted. On the one hand, I'm bothered when people come up to me. I wish I didn't have to deal with them. On the other hand, I feel like I need to do *something* to help. I even feel guilty if I don't. After all, Jesus met the needs of many who begged him for help, and didn't the Good Samaritan stop to help the man beaten on the side of the road (unlike the Levite and priest who passed him by)? Overlaying all of this is the incredible complexity of the situation. What actually *helps* in a situation like this?

Whether to offer money or not is a complex, nuanced question (and I'm going to frustrate you further by not answering it completely), but I've realized over time that I at least need a way to respond so I don't totally dismiss people. What's helped is for me to simply ask them a question in reply.

It's a simple one. I'll merely say, "I'm David; what's your name?"

It's been amazing to see what happens when I ask people their name. At first, they are surprised—because people rarely ask them their name. And then it makes them feel seen. There's a measure of value when we call one another by our names. It acknowledges the uniqueness of each of us as individuals.

From there, the moment can go in lots of directions. I'll ask them what their situation is and what they need. Usually it's a short conversation. Often it's still very awkward and uncomfortable. But it's one in which I hope a measure of dignity and respect is conveyed to them.

Remember Don, my Kudzu Village friend? I realized that my biggest challenge with him at first was seeing his value and worth. I judged him based on his appearance and looked down on him because of the choices he had made in his life. When I became his mentor during the Jobs for Life class, my role was called a "champion." In other words, I was supposed to be his biggest fan, the one who would always have his back. No matter what he faced, he had someone in his corner who believed in him and thought the world of him.

Really, we should all have someone like that in our lives. After all, every single person on earth is made in the image of God. Everyone you meet, however incredible or annoying or confusing, reflects some aspect of who God is. We all are of inestimable worth.

Just leaders see that value and worth in others—and they communicate that value often.

3. Their Flaws and Failures: At this point, you might think I'm being overly optimistic, even naïve. *It's all well and good,* you may think, *to treat people with dignity. But we have to be realistic, too: People can be pretty messed up!*

To which I say, "Good point."

Seeing others for who they are doesn't mean we squint our eyes so their flaws and failures disappear. Shay, for instance, wasn't perfect. I wouldn't have done her any favors by pretending her flaws didn't exist. But just leaders refuse to let flaws and failures define another person's existence.

I just mentioned that every person you meet bears the image of God. They have an air of divinity about them. But there's a flip side to this, too. Everyone you meet was also made from dust (see Genesis 2). They are sinful. They've done wrong. They've made mistakes.

Divine *and* dusty. Full of potential and haunted by sin. Sound complicated? That's the human condition.

If you find it difficult to hold these two truths in tension, just take a look at yourself. If you're self-aware, you should know *a lot* about the flaws and failures of the person looking back at you in the mirror. Does that make you write that person off? Usually not. You're able to recognize your own flaws *along with* all of the value and worth.

We all carry in our lives both incredible beauty and deep brokenness. It's tempting to hide our weaknesses, but we all have them, and we need to see them in those we lead—not as a way to elevate ourselves over others, but as a way to empathize and experience solidarity with one another. Divine and dusty—that's all of us.

4. Their Fears: Kudzu Village Don decided to take the Jobs for Life class *despite his fears*. Little did I know how fearful he was. On the first day of class, he didn't show. Class was about to begin . . . no Don.

As his champion, I was trained to do all I could to make sure he was there. So I ran out of the church to go and find him. And sure enough, as I started down the sidewalk, I could see Don running toward me, looking worried and a bit out of sorts.

When he hurriedly entered the classroom, he apologized to everyone for his tardiness. He told us he had been vomiting back in his room because he was so scared to come to class.

Well, that endeared Don to all of us. His willingness to share his fear made us love him all the more. It also encouraged everyone else to be free to share their fears.

I'm a pretty confident guy. I don't normally operate from a place of fear. Unless I'm way up high looking over a ledge or confronting a mouse (it's legit, OK?), I'm usually pretty good at controlling my fears. I'll bet if you're a leader, you may have a good handle on your fears, too.

It's difficult for people like me to sympathize with others who struggle with fear. But many people have fears. They're real. And they matter.

The challenge for a just leader is to know when to push people to face their fears and when to simply accept them. At times, leadership means nudging people along, coaching them to greater courage, helping them to overcome their fears. At times, leadership means waiting for a more opportune time. At times, leadership means putting people in positions where they aren't face-to-face with their fears in unhealthy ways. It's tough to know when to push and when to wait. But good leaders are always striving to get that balance right.

5. Their Dreams: When I was young, I dreamed of playing basketball for the University of North Carolina. I was a good basketball player, having played all my life and for my high school team. But it was a long shot. After all, this was the UNC Tar Heels, one of the most storied basketball teams in the country. I was six feet nothin' and *slowwwww*. But I could shoot. So, my dream lived on.

What are your dreams? Where do you see yourself in five to ten years? Can you envision it? Do your dreams drive what you do today? Do you share them with others? And do you ask others to share their dreams with you?

The day I entered into a game with North Carolina emblazoned across my jersey was the day my dream finally came true. I was a sophomore at UNC and had made the JV basketball team.

Now, you may be thinking, *Isn't JV a high school thing?* And you're right: UNC is one of the only major universities with a JV program. Even the JV squad was tough, though. I had tried out my freshman year, but I got cut at the final cut.

The next year, however, I had the tryout of my life, and I made the team! Everyone who knows me knows that was a defining experience of my life. The accomplishment, the hard work, the experiences, and relationships I made were life-changing for me.

Did I go on to become a professional basketball player? Obviously not. But pursuing one dream gave me confidence to pursue other dreams down the line.

Our dreams drive us. That was true of my UNC basketball dream. It's true of you and your dreams. And it's true of everyone you meet. Most of us don't take the time to learn about the dreams bouncing around in the hearts of other people.

But just leaders aren't most people. Take the time. Learn about the dreams of others. You'll be glad you did.

WHAT THE BEST "SEERS" DO

I want to end this chapter with something super practical. It's relatively easy to talk about what we *should* be seeing in others. But for most of us, this isn't natural or easy.

I include myself in that number. Seeing others in all of their nuance and complexity is something I *learned* to do over the course of years. (Still learning, by the way.) If you're like me, you might benefit from a few "best practices." Seeing others may not be natural for you, but it's something you can learn to do—and even learn to do *well*. In my experience, those who see others are masters at six things:

1. They are curious about others. I grew up passionately devoted to UNC basketball. At no point in my childhood did someone need to sit me down and say, "All right, David, this is how you learn about UNC hoops." Nope. Not even a little necessary. I was curious about everything UNC did *because I loved UNC.*

While good techniques can help you learn about other people, nothing beats an abundance of curiosity. And nothing drives curiosity like love.

2. They ask great questions. We all ask questions. But far too many of us keep the questions at the surface level. *Where are you from? What do you do? What are your plans for this weekend?* All of that is fine. But if you want to see people at a deeper level, you need to ask deeper questions.

Now, don't be flippant here. Asking deep questions is an art, and you can do some real damage by asking everyone you meet about their greatest fears. But do some work to get a layer or two beneath the surface. Practice asking people about their dreams about the future. Ask them about their story. Or simply invite them in by asking, "What do you think?"

3. They listen attentively. The best questions in the world won't do you any good if you zone out as soon as the other person begins speaking. To *see* people well, you need to *listen* well. Practically, this probably means following the advice you got from your mom: Look people in the eye; nod along as they speak; don't interrupt. You may be surprised how much trust you can build simply by being a good listener.

4. They are fully present. How do you feel when you're talking with someone else . . . and suddenly, they break eye contact, turn to their phone, and start typing?

I'm going to guess: *not great.*

Our powers of perception take a huge nosedive when we're distracted. So, when you're with other people, be there—be all there. Put your phone away. It's just one way we can practice the Golden Rule: "Listen to others the way you want them to listen to you."

5. They follow through. Just leaders do what they say they're going to do. We all know people who say one thing and do another. They tell us they will get back to us . . . and never do. They say they will have an answer by a certain date . . . and we never hear from them, so we end up writing them off.

Just leaders, instead, pay attention and remember the important dates in people's lives; they meet the deadlines; they make good on what they said they were going to do.

They under-promise and over-deliver.

For example, one area I've really needed to work on to be this kind of leader is remembering people's birthdays.

Birthdays are interesting. People usually don't *tell* others it's their birthday, but they desperately want others to *know* it's their birthday. Understanding this, I have made it a habit to put in my calendar the birthdays of all those close to me—family, friends, colleagues. I get a reminder a few days ahead of time so I'm ready to send them a message or card on their big day.

Nothing about this process is novel or groundbreaking. I simply made a system (and a pretty mundane one, at that) to remember birthdays. And yet, I can't tell you how many times people have responded with overwhelming thanks. My little system nudges me in the direction of a habit I want—following through—because I've learned that a small intentional gesture can go a long way.

6. They aren't in a rush. Seeing others in all of their nuance and complexity takes time. For most of us, we simply don't have it. Or if you're like me, you're so focused on your own tasks that you can't stand to be interrupted. We can be too focused or in too much of a rush to notice when someone isn't doing well or is uncomfortable. We don't have time to ask about someone's story because we've got work to do, deadlines to meet, and emails to respond to.

I'm not suggesting you avoid your email and spend all of your waking hours in leisurely conversations with people. I am, however, suggesting that your pace will determine what you see. Rush by other people, and you won't ever see them. Slow down and listen? Worlds unfold before you.

WHAT YOU SEE DETERMINES WHAT YOU GET

Hiring Shay was one of the best decisions of my life. She started in an administrative role for twenty-five hours a week and quickly moved into a full-time role. She absolutely transformed our culture, and her energy took JfL to a whole new level.

In time, Shay ended up being our director of training, traveling all over the country to train leaders to equip them to lead JfL classes.

And to think, I almost missed out on all of that. We almost missed out on all of that.

There's a kind of irony when it comes to seeing others: What you see determines what you get. If all you see is problems and flaws, that's likely all you'll ever get. But if you see potential, value, and dreams? Don't be surprised when that's what you end up getting.

In Shay, what I saw determined what I got—an extraordinary teammate and a lifelong friend.

QUESTIONS TO CONSIDER

1. Who are the people you are leading or with whom you have influence?
2. What steps have you taken to know them?
3. What steps do you need to take to know them better?
4. What implicit biases do you need to overcome to see people for who they really are?

CHAPTER 7

What We Need to See in Our Community

In April 2019, Raleigh, North Carolina, where I live, received another accolade as a city. Raleigh often is in the Top 10 of best places to live in America, much to the delight of our Chamber of Commerce. This time the city was ranked third in the world for the best quality of life. The only cities ahead of us were Canberra in Australia and Eindhoven in the Netherlands. According to Numbeo, the world's largest cost of living database, Raleigh has the best quality of life in the United States.[22]

That same week, the *New York Times* ran an article entitled "The Neighborhood Is Mostly Black. The Home Buyers Are Mostly White," exposing the growing gentrification and lack of affordable housing . . . in Raleigh.[23] At the time of the article, Raleigh was short sixty thousand affordable housing units.

In fact, according to the Equality of Opportunity Project, out of America's one hundred largest cities, when ranked on the possibility of upward mobility, Raleigh ranked ninety-fifth. In other words, if you are born poor in Raleigh, you have an extremely high likelihood of remaining poor.[24] You could count on one hand the cities that fared worse.

So, which Raleigh do I live in? The one with the highest quality of life in the United States? Or the one with one of the lowest rates of affordable housing and nearly no chance of upward mobility? Is Raleigh flourishing . . . or fractured?

This problem may be acute in Raleigh. But trust me, my city isn't an outlier here. Most American cities exhibit this kind of Jekyll-and-Hyde reality. To say the least, it's incredibly disorienting.

It is easy to compartmentalize my world and only see one part of my community—the one I prefer or feel most connected to or comfortable in. I can go days, weeks, or even months not seeing or experiencing the tougher side of my city. I can keep believing that I live in the best city in the nation. But "my Raleigh" isn't the whole picture. For thousands of others, Raleigh is rough. Thriving seems impossible. Opportunity is distant.

If you're born materially poor and you live in a place where you are likely to remain poor, but that place is considered to have *the best quality of life in the world,* how are you supposed to feel? Seen? Understood? Recognized? Valued?

Or discouraged? Overlooked? Hopeless? Discarded?

Just leaders see and are intimately connected with *all* parts of their community. They do not choose to see one side while neglecting the other. They are intentional to see the whole community—the messy, confusing, disorienting, real-life whole.

A MOUNTAINTOP VIEW

When you read the Gospel narratives about Jesus—especially the miracle stories—it's easy to miss some of the smaller details. After all, *Jesus is doing miracles,* for crying out loud. But the surrounding context of his miracles often has a lot to teach us.

Here's one example that reveals not only *what* Jesus was doing, but *where*:

> Jesus went on from there and walked beside the Sea of Galilee. And he went up on the mountain and sat down there. And great crowds came to him, bringing with them the lame, the blind, the crippled, the mute, and many others, and they put them at his feet, and he healed them, so that

the crowd wondered, when they saw the mute speaking, the crippled healthy, the lame walking, and the blind seeing. And they glorified the God of Israel. (Matthew 15:29–31)

Jesus was constantly climbing up mountains. Part of that is theological: He was showing himself to be a truer and better Moses, who went up the mountain to receive and proclaim God's law (see Matthew 5—7). But part of that is much more basic and practical: Jesus went up the mountain for greater access. He could teach more people from there. He could see more people from there. The mountaintop view gave him a broader perspective.

To see the whole community, our position matters. Like Jesus, we need to put ourselves in places where we have a broad picture of the whole community. We need a mountaintop view. Of course, we may not literally climb a mountain to get that view. But the principle remains: To see what no one else is seeing, we need to go where no one else is going.

As we seek to become leaders who see our community with clarity, here are three primary steps we can take:

1. Know the History of Your Community: Just like seeing ourselves and others, just leaders pay careful attention to the history of the community in which they live and work. They understand the events and decisions made in the past that give context to what is taking place today. Every city and community has a story—how it started, who were the key players, what businesses took shape, how the city was laid out, what fueled the neighborhoods, how politics evolved, what events had the greatest impact.

Visionary leaders in the city next to us, Durham, North Carolina, created the Durham Pilgrimage of Pain and Hope, a two-day experience to help people understand the unique history of the community. Participants visit various sites and listen to city leaders who share the key events and issues that have shaped the city's story. And as the title suggests, it lets people see and understand the pain that is a part of the city's story as well as what has provided hope. Some years later, their model led leaders in Raleigh to create a similar pilgrimage for our city.

What sorts of things do we need to know about the history of our communities? Ask questions like these:

- What led to this city's founding? Who was involved? (Who *wasn't*?)
- How did business and industry develop? Who was in power? (Again . . . who *wasn't*?)
- How were neighborhoods formed? What injustices took place? What were the key institutions?
- Who were the influential leaders? What motivated them? What challenges had to be overcome?

If you don't know the history of your community, you can start today. Become a student of your city, asking the kinds of questions normally reserved for a curious visitor: Why is your city set up the way it is? Why do people live in certain areas and others live elsewhere? Why do some schools have resources and others don't? Why are streets and buildings named the way they are? Why do certain people and institutions have influence, while others are overlooked?

Knowing the history of a community gives context for what we see and experience today. It helps us see its richness, depth, and complexity. And while this history is often difficult, it leads us to an important place: we soon realize that the issues we face aren't as simple and straightforward as they seem.

2. Go to (and Spend Time in) the Places You Don't Know: Just leaders are intentional about exposing themselves to people and places in their city that are often overlooked. They know the neighborhoods, the streets, the businesses, the churches, the schools, the parks, the food, the people, etc. And I mean *know* them—not as spots on a map, but as places they've personally been.

Of course, just leaders aren't going to know everything about a particular community, but they intentionally go out of their way to shop at the businesses, go to the restaurants, or attend the events to get to know the community and the people who live and work there. As my friend Pastor Jerome Gay puts it, they practice "intentional displacement." They aren't visitors to those "other" parts of town; they are integrated members of the community.

Stop for a moment and think about your city. What parts of town are blank spaces on your mental map? Where, if you ventured there, would you feel a bit out of place, like a visitor or a cultural outsider? (You can't spend time in new places if you don't pause long enough to figure out which ones they are!)

Just leaders don't see parts of their community as "them," "over there," or "those people." Instead, they think "we," "ours," and "us." They have a deep belonging to all parts of their community and take the time to get to know it and immerse themselves in the places and cultures they don't usually see. They adopt the community as their own and take keen interest in any changes that are forthcoming in the community. They are quick to observe subtle changes occurring within the community that signal larger opportunities and challenges.

I want to encourage you: One of the first steps you can take to be a just leader is simply to take a drive around your city (or better yet, a walk!) in particular places you rarely go. Practice "intentional displacement," putting yourself in situations where you are the cultural outlier. And then, take note of what you see, the slower the better.

3. Get Close to Those in Need: Just leaders are also intentional about connecting to those who are hurting and in need—the quartet of the vulnerable that we mentioned earlier (orphans, widows, immigrants, and the poor). After all, that's what *mishpat* is all about. In order for us to be just, we have to put ourselves in close proximity to people in need—not merely to serve them, but to *know* them, build mutual relationships with them, and understand their unique gifts and talents and the barriers they face.

This sounds great on paper, but it may seem impossible to do—especially for someone like you. I get it: If you are a busy leader, trying to stay above water with your work and business, taking care of your family, and meeting the needs and expectations people have of you, how is it even conceivable for you to engage people in need in a meaningful way? When would you make the time?

This is hard to do when you feel obligated to do it. It's much easier, however, when you realize that *you need it*. Remember what we said earlier: Engaging people in need is the means through which God fulfills our deepest needs. When we live with those in need, God promises to make our bones strong, to make us a well-watered garden, to satisfy our needs. He transforms us from fractured to flourishing. Don't you want that? Don't you need it?

You make time for the things you need. And you need to spend time with people who are materially poor and hurting.

What might that look like?

- Pick a new restaurant (or new barber, or new grocery store) in a different part of town. Start with something small, but try to make it a regular habit.
- Identify a school in a low-income area of your city, then see what opportunities you and/or your business can do to support them.
- See what the local county, chamber of commerce, or Parks and Rec departments offer. Pick a program for you—and even your family—to participate in. Consider offering a training in an area where there is a need and you have experience.
- Get to know a leader of a local nonprofit organization in your community that serves people in material need. Offer to take them to lunch to learn more about them and hear their expertise around the particular needs they are addressing. Be a student of their work.

These are just a few ideas to help jump-start your mind. There are lots of others you could pursue. Just remember that time with those in material need is a place you will see and experience God in profound ways.

WHAT THE BEST "SEERS" WILL SEE IN THEIR COMMUNITY

If you take the time to learn the history of your city, go to places where you're the cultural outsider, and get close to the hurting, odds are you're going to encounter a number of difficult issues—poverty, homelessness, unemployment, education disparities. But if you're truly opening your eyes to see your city, these "issues"—which I'm sure you've heard of and I'm confident you have opinions about—will become more than issues. They will take on flesh. It's the difference between seeing a faded picture of the Grand Canyon and visiting yourself. What exists now in your 2D mental model will be painted in—and sometimes changed by—the 3D reality.

You might be surprised at what you find.

Just leaders see at least five things as they begin to look at their community around them.

1. **Reality is not what it seems.** It's easy to judge from afar. It's also easy to think we know what poor communities need—even though we know very little about them and have hardly ever set foot in them! The solutions, we believe, are simple. All they need to do is (*fill in the blank*), and the problems will magically go away.

Once you get close to the people and the places where they live, though, reality is often not what you thought. Not only do you realize that the challenges and issues are much more complex and nuanced, but you begin to see people's giftedness rather than their shortcomings, their assets and not their liabilities.

It's quite humbling and convicting. Your arrogance is exposed. At least, mine often is.

When our kids were in middle school, we happened to be zoned for one of the lowest-performing middle schools in our city. Our school was not located in a poorer part of town, but people had stopped sending their kids there, and the school developed a reputation as a bad school that was unsafe. After elementary school, where most everyone sent their children to their neighborhood school, people scattered and made lots of different choices for their children during middle school. Very few chose to stay in the low-performing middle school in our neighborhood.

We were one of those few families. Despite its reputation, we learned very quickly the school was not what it appeared from the outside. Did it have issues? Absolutely—just like all middle schools. But the leaders and the teachers at the school showed the same amount of love, attention, and care as those at any other school. There were challenges, but we joined in on those challenges, and our kids developed a deep appreciation for people not like them and built lifelong friendships that have helped them see and experience a big God.

2. People in marginalized communities are experts. Usually, when we engage poor communities, we go there with the mindset that we are there to help. We have resources, poor communities lack resources, and we are there to provide the resources and the know-how to make their communities better. When we operate in this mindset, we overlook the profound wisdom, resources, and giftedness in these communities. In every community, there are people whose lived experience is nothing short of extraordinary: people who have overcome seemingly insurmountable odds, people who know how to survive, persevere, make lemonade out of lemons, and cling to hope.

They have a wealth of knowledge and experience, and we need every bit of it. So, instead of coming in with our resources to help, we need to sit at their feet and learn from them.

I have taken several of my business groups to sit and learn from my friend Pastor Phillip Walker of Mt. Pleasant Worship and Outreach Center, a predominantly African American church on Sawyer Road near downtown Raleigh. Phillip has been the pastor for more than thirty years, and his relatively small church has had a tremendous impact on the community, though many people outside the community might not realize it.

At the time he started his church, Sawyer Road was one of the most dangerous streets in our city—full of crime, drugs, prostitution, and economic and spiritual poverty. Phillip tells the story of preaching one Sunday morning and seeing from the pulpit gang activity taking place right outside the sanctuary's clear glass windows.

Phillip and the leaders of the church began to address these issues through a variety of initiatives—job training for young people involved in or at risk of joining gangs; soccer and midnight basketball leagues; after-school tutoring; housing and employment for drug dealers; and financial management classes.

They also led the effort to designate approximately ten blocks around the church as a "Weed and Seed" site. This strategy from the US Department of Justice "weeds" out the neighborhood criminal elements through law enforcement and "seeds" the neighborhoods with economic and social reform.

Phillip and leaders in his church anticipated the changing dynamics in the community over the last several years. As development began to take place downtown, neighborhood property values skyrocketed, and longstanding residents of the community were being displaced due to gentrification.

As a result, they formed Mt. Pleasant Ventures, through which they were able to acquire and rehabilitate Shammah Winds Apartments, an apartment complex just across the street from their church. This property had been the epicenter of violence, prostitution, and illegal drug sales within the community. The three-million-dollar acquisition and rehab project provided stable affordable housing for thirty-two families.

Currently, they are working on a thirteen-million-dollar project called Summit at Sawyer, utilizing Low-Income Housing Tax Credits to build 150 units of affordable housing right next to Shammah Winds Apartments.

Phillip and the leaders of his church have become experts in affordable housing development, tax credits, and church/city partnerships. They are addressing the physical, emotional, and spiritual needs of people who have experienced trauma. They are leading the way in thinking creatively about ways to access resources and affordable housing (a critical issue, as we know from the beginning of this chapter) to address the needs of a community. It's incredible.

And after watching him for years, I'm not even sure I've seen *half* of what he's done.

3. Economic poverty is often offset by relational wealth. In my work with business leaders, I have come across something both fascinating and troubling—the "poverty of wealth": people who have influence and power and all the money they could ever want and yet are miserable. They are stressed out, anxious, and bored, with frayed marriages, little margin, no exercise, very little sleep, and isolated from relationships.

We have been conditioned to be self-sufficient, independent people who can take care of ourselves. The result isn't pretty.

On the other hand, in poor communities, I have experienced something equally as surprising—wealth that comes from authentic relationships and a deep dependence upon one another. Deep dependence and deep compassion go hand in hand, because when we're all battling together, we are moved to care for the needs of others. The result is richness.

Thelma was a single mom in Memphis who experienced something no mother should ever have to endure—the loss of her three sons. One was stillborn. Another went to prison at fifteen and was poisoned there. The third was shot and killed when he was seventeen. I interviewed her because, in her grief, she was able to meet the young man who had killed her seventeen-year-old-son and offer forgiveness to him.

In the course of telling me this story, Thelma pointed to a young woman who was sitting with her children not far away. She proceeded to tell me how she had taken the young woman and her children into her home. The woman had fallen on hard times and needed a place to stay to get back on her feet.

I was dumbfounded. Despite her own trauma and lack of resources, Thelma did not think twice about taking this woman and her children into her home. If it were me, I would have wondered what the impact of doing something like this would have on my life and family. Would we still be able to do the things we want to do? How much money would it cost? What issues would we have to deal with? For Thelma, those questions were hardly relevant. She viewed the woman and her children as family, and she was not going to turn her back on family.

Family is wealth. And in poorer communities, I often see a much greater sense of family. I see people who are struggling together and therefore understand what one another is going through. People who need one another to survive. Most of us long for that—we desperately need it—yet we often remain in our own bubbles of self-sufficiency. And we're miserable.

4. Joy is plentiful. Many of us tend to assume that joy is the result of a life gone right. If life has dealt us good cards, we should be happy. If our hand doesn't look that great, then of course we'll be miserable.

The reality isn't quite that simple.

Yes, there are tremendous difficulties for those living in poverty. I don't want to idealize that painful experience. But my experience and the testimony of Scripture reveal a surprising pattern: People hardened by struggle often know true joy.

Joy is different from happiness. Happiness really is a circumstantial thing. The etymology of the word itself even points this direction; it originally meant "lucky" or "successful." Joy isn't like that. Joy can exist regardless of the circumstances. So, whether times are thick or thin, you either have joy . . . or you don't.

I'll admit, it is difficult to have joy with a lived experience steeped in pain and suffering. But be honest with yourself: How many truly joyful people do you know who live in prosperity?

When I talk with people who go on mission trips to developing countries around the world, their number one reaction is always the impact of seeing the joy people in poverty have despite their circumstances. It's unnerving and convicting. And, honestly, it's compelling: When you have joy, it's a bright light beaming to all those around you.

To a certain extent, I can anesthetize myself from struggle—either through the resources I have or the comforts I pursue. Doing that may make me happy for a time, but it does not lead to joy. Joy is built on hope, a longing for God, and an understanding of his goodness all around me, no matter what I'm experiencing.

So, here's my counterintuitive advice: If you need joy, spend time close to those in need. It's just the kind of disorientation your soul needs.

5. Access and opportunity are a relationship away. Typically, we come into communities to help—to offer people a "hand up" so their circumstances can get better. That's not a terrible starting point. But even better than a "hand up" is a "hand across"—coming in to build a relationship. Build one with a person in the community who has trust, experience, and can help open your eyes to its beauty and opportunities. Elevate and support the work already taking place. Don't take credit. Decrease so that others increase.

Relationships take time. You don't come in with an agenda. You just show up . . . and you keep showing up. Remember, communities in need aren't looking for you to do drive-bys, but they are eager for you to come in and stay.

That's not to say the *only* thing you bring is your friendship (though that is the most valuable thing!). The friendship can function as a bridge, providing access and opportunities to people and networks who are overlooked.

Take Ken and Beverly Jenkins, for instance. They had a vision. The shopping center in their community had been vacant for almost twenty years. As pastors of Refuge and Restoration Ministries, Ken and Beverly saw an opportunity, but there were many obstacles. The center was in the heart of Dellwood, Missouri. It had become an eyesore and a picture of de-investment in the community as shopping centers and strip malls were left barren.

Of course, the riots outside the complex didn't help.

Why all the uproar? On August 9, 2014, in a small suburb of St. Louis, police officer Darren Wilson had shot and killed Michael Brown, an unarmed Black teenager. That small suburb was Ferguson, Missouri—just a few blocks from Dellwood and the shopping center.

Protests and riots ensued in Ferguson, in Dellwood, and eventually in cities all across the country. The shooting ignited long-simmering tensions between the majority-Black population of Ferguson and the local police, who were mostly White. Ferguson was in the news for all the wrong reasons.

These challenges did not deter Ken and Beverly. In fact, they added fuel to their fire. If there was ever a time to invest in the community, it was now. But they had to be creative. There was a ton of attention on Ferguson and the surrounding communities because of what happened, but resources and ideas to solve the problems were coming from people *outside* of the community with mixed agendas. Some wanted to take advantage of what was going on to fund their projects, while others just wanted to make all of the problems go away, and fast.

Ken and Beverly knew they had to take the time necessary to understand the needs of the community, listen to the people, and build a plan that would not only meet the needs of the people but be financially sustainable. They discovered the shopping center was owned by a man in Chicago who had very little interest in the community. Maybe they could buy it . . .

It would cost millions of dollars to purchase it from him, and much more to renovate it with the services it could provide.

Ken and Beverly had never raised that sum of money. They had never even considered it. They were not deterred. Still, they had no idea where the money might come from.

Meanwhile, a man named John Ross was deeply concerned about the strife and pain within the city of Ferguson. He was a long-time resident of St. Louis and had built a thriving and impactful real estate business. As a man with resources, he wanted to help, but he didn't know how.

Usually, people like John could just apply their business acumen to solve the problem, but this was much more complex, and even though John was a man of influence, he had no influence in Ferguson. No one knew him. And because no one knew him, no one would have trusted him.

Through a friend, he heard about a Bible study being led by a pastor from the community, Ken Jenkins, to help leaders in the city understand how to cross racial divides. He had never experienced such a study but given the circumstances with the riots and the racial unrest, it was timely. Through the Bible study, Ken and John developed a close friendship. They spent time outside of the study getting to know one another and hearing each other's hearts. Eventually, John realized that Ken had a deeper vision for the community than he was letting on. John asked him about it.

It was then that John realized how he could help.

Jump ahead to the ribbon cutting ceremony, nine years later. Yes, I said *nine years*. Ken and Beverly celebrated with many partners, including John, who had come together sharing their time, resources, and wisdom to put together the R&R Marketplace, an $18 million, self-sustaining development. R&R Marketplace turned the vacant shopping center into a multifaceted complex containing an early childhood education center, a workforce training center, an innovation center (co-working facility), a bank, a health center, a church, a restaurant, and more. Within the first five years, more than two thousand people are expected to become employed through the training offered.

All because some folks took the time to look around.

Jesus was a master at seeing. When he looked at others, he did not just see them—he knew them. Like a shepherd looks at his sheep. Like a mother looks at her children. Like God looks at you and me.

Seeing isn't easy. Often, what we see breaks our heart. But we follow a God who binds up what is broken. And in the end, when we see with his eyes, we begin to hear his heartbeat as well. We learn what Ken and Beverly and John learned—that the more we see, the more we become just. The more we become just, the more we thrive.

And eventually, what we'll see—in ourselves, in others, in our community—will look quite a bit more beautiful.

QUESTIONS TO CONSIDER

1. How would you describe your community/city?
2. What do you love about your community/city?
3. What's the history of your community/city? What steps do you need to take to get to know its history better?
4. How should the connection to your community/city impact your leadership?

BUILD CULTURAL COMPETENCY

David Foster Wallace, at the graduation of the Kenyon College class of 2005, told this parable:

> There are these two young fish swimming along, and they happen to meet an older fish swimming the other way, who nods at them and says, "Morning, boys. How's the water?" And the two young fish swim on for a bit, and then eventually one of them looks over at the other and goes, "What the hell is water?"[25]

Do you know that there is water all around you? OK, not actual water. But the water of culture.

Culture is a pretty slippery word. Many of us don't even realize we *have* a culture, especially if we're White. Culture is what influences *other* groups of people. But me? The way I see the world? Well, that's the way the world actually is.

It would be a great step forward for all of us to realize that we're much more like Wallace's fish than we'd care to admit. We are all incredibly steeped in beliefs, practices, and assumptions that shape our view of the world. We are steeped in a culture every bit as immersive as an ocean is to a fish.

Our choice isn't *whether* we swim in a culture or not. It's whether we acknowledge it or not. And then, it's what we do with that knowledge. Leaders who can understand culture will flourish—as will those around them. Leaders who can't will struggle—as will those around them.

In the following chapters, we'll take a look at cultural competency (what is it and why it matters) and then address several areas where just leaders need to have cultural competency in the twenty-first century—race, poverty, and sexuality and gender. We'll close by looking at the most culturally competent leader in history.

CHAPTER 8

What Is Cultural Competency?

"I'm good enough, I'm smart enough, and doggone it, people like me." If you are a fan of *Saturday Night Live*, you know who said this phrase: Stuart Smalley. Played by Al Franken, Stuart aired a segment called *Daily Affirmation*, a mock self-help show that appeared for the first time in 1991.[26]

The show opened with Stuart saying positive reinforcement messages to himself: "I deserve good things; I'm entitled to my share of happiness; I refuse to beat myself up; I am an attractive person; I am fun to be with."

The sketch was a spoof on the growing self-help programs that were starting to become popular at the time. Seemingly unaware of their fame, Stuart would have well-known guests join him, the sorts of people at the peak of their '90s fame—Macaulay Culkin, Roseanne Barr, Michael Jordan. Even though they were on screen, Stuart would use pseudonyms to "protect their identity." Then he would spend the time affirming this ridiculously successful person, assuming they were filled with self-doubt. Stuart wanted to make sure that they knew how valuable they really were . . . even though, of course, they already knew that.

Each show would end with Stuart looking into a mirror (or, even better, forcing his guest to look into the mirror) and reciting the phrase, "I'm good enough, I'm smart enough, and doggone it, people like me."

WHAT IS CULTURAL COMPETENCY?

It's pretty easy for us to take a look at someone like Michael Jordan and say, "That guy has value." Six-time NBA champ, five-time league MVP, holder of more records than most of us (even fans) can recall. Clearly, Jordan doesn't need anyone like Stuart Smalley reminding him that he's got value and dignity.

But nearly everyone we meet does. That's the ironic truth embedded in Stuart Smalley's sketch: Self-help methods might not always work, but they tap into something we deeply need—an affirmation of our value.

As we begin the discussion of cultural competency, it's important to note that the core of being culturally competent is the *imago Dei*: recognizing that everyone is made in the image of God and has unique value and dignity. While that means everyone has extraordinary worth and value, it also means each of us carry with us aspects of God in our vast array of color, personalities, gifts, and talents. God *intended* the diversity of ethnicities and cultures we experience today. The more we press into them, the more we understand God and his identity.

Cultural competency, in short, is the ability to affirm, build trust with, and effectively engage people across different cultures.

This is no easy task. But for a just leader, it's indispensable. To thrive in today's world, we must be able to both *value* the cultural diversity around us and *seamlessly navigate* cross-cultural situations. Just leaders are always diving deeper into culture—both their own and that of others. It's a dive well worth the effort, especially in today's increasingly diverse world.

WHY DOES CULTURAL COMPETENCY MATTER FOR LEADERS?

1. Cultural competency is important to God. The picture of God's Kingdom begins in Genesis when he creates humanity in his image (see Genesis 1:27) and ends in Revelation with people across all nations and tongues worshiping around God's throne—a great multitude that no one could count, from every nation, tribe, people and language, standing before the throne and before the Lamb (see Revelation 7).

All of us, in the flavors and colors we embody, reflect the Creator of the Universe, and our future is an eternal reality of worshiping him with all of our diversity.

This kind of cultural diversity wasn't just limited to the bookends of the Bible, though. Jesus himself modeled cultural competency throughout his life, too. He was a master at crossing cultural, racial, social, ethnic, political, economic, and gender lines.

It's one of the reasons no one could quite figure him out. We will see this played out in detail in Chapter 12 as we unpack Jesus's interaction with the woman at the well. He seemed at home with the poor *and* the rich, among men *and* women, with Jews and Gentiles, in the homes of leaders *and* on the streets with outcasts.

If we limit ourselves to thinking of God without a broad view of culture, we will have a very small picture of who God is and what he is all about. On the other hand, the more we know of culture, the more we know of God.

2. Cultural plurality is the future. As our nation becomes more ethnically diverse, twenty-first-century leaders need to know how to navigate various cultures well. To do otherwise is, even just from a business standpoint, foolish.

DEI (Diversity, Equity, and Inclusion) initiatives in the marketplace have expanded rapidly as companies recognize the need to create workplace cultures that allow all people to thrive. Leaders are realizing they can no longer consider this peripheral or optional. While it's important to understand how to address DEI initiatives effectively, large companies have been on the forefront of this growth for a couple reasons: 1) they have the resources to fund them, and 2) they sense the need to demonstrate to the public that this is a priority to them. (Granted, not every large company has been equally sincere in these efforts; as always, it's easier to say the right things than to affect true, top-to-bottom change.)

Smaller, private companies are more of a mixed bag. Typically, their attentiveness to issues of culture are driven by the particular work they do, what their employee base is, whether they have had an incident that has forced them to engage with it, or the interest and passion of their leadership. Since few small companies have diverse workforces, they often consider cultural competency as outside their core business.

That could not be further from the truth.

World-class leaders must build cultural competency or they will be left behind. Just like any emerging market—say, new technologies, the growth of carbon, even new currencies—we make leadership decisions today to be ready for what's ahead tomorrow. Just leaders, after all, aren't content to see what everyone else sees. They want to look further down the road.

Wouldn't we rather lead in the future than cling to what leadership looked like in the past? To thrive in a culturally diverse world rather than hide from it?

BUILDING CULTURAL COMPETENCY IS HARD AND TAKES TIME

Building cultural competency is not an easy venture. I was with a group of young leaders recently, talking about this. I put up a PowerPoint slide for us to discuss. On it were pictures of various groups of people holding signs:

- "Black Lives Matter."
- "Police Lives Matter."
- "All Lives Matter."
- "White Silence Equals Violence."
- "Trans Lives Matter."

I said, "Whether you asked for it or not, this is your generation's challenge—navigating the complex world of culture that will only become more difficult through the years."

Then I asked them a series of questions:

- Is it OK to say, "Black lives matter?" What about, "Blue lives matter?" Are there times when saying either of these might not be wise or compassionate?
- Can we say, "All lives matter?" And if we can, are there times when it might be *inappropriate* to say it?
- What about "Trans lives matter?" Is that OK to say? What are the unique challenges of understanding how our society is navigating gender issues and treating them as part of culture?

And finally, I asked these young leaders, most of whom were White, "How many of you feel pressure from your friends to post something on social media after a police shooting of an unarmed Black man or any other prominent act of injustice?"

Ninety-five percent of the hands shot up.

Even if they did not know what to say, these leaders felt the pressure not to be silent (like the sign suggested: "White silence equals violence"). They did not want to be categorized as not being *woke* (a term that signifies someone who is culturally aware—i.e., has *woken* up to the cultural issues at hand).

This kind of pressure can be exhausting. People are frustrated. If they say something, it's wrong; if they remain silent, it's wrong. Social media makes it worse as people shout their viewpoints in a vacuum and force people to take sides.

A quick word of advice: Social media may be good for a lot of things, but it's a rough place to engage in conversations related to justice, race, and culture. It's impersonal. It's not relational. There's no dialogue or understanding of tone and intent. It can do more damage than good. I won't say it's impossible to have fruitful conversations there. It's just a tremendously uphill climb, with increasingly minimal chances of success.

So, if you feel pressure to post something on social media after a current event, don't. Only post something *because you feel the freedom to post*, not to measure up to the expectations you feel people have of you.

In addition, feel the freedom that comes with engaging these issues *in person*, with small groups of people where you have the opportunity to build relationships and engage with one another over the long haul. That is the best context in which you can be safe to disagree and question one another while moving *toward* one another instead of apart.

Remember: God created culture, but he *is* justice. So as we strive to be just leaders who follow him, we can have a healthy perspective and motivation to cross cultural lines. We aren't doing it to be relevant or woke or to avoid being canceled. We're doing it to embody the gospel. Jesus crossed a huge gap by becoming one of us, God becoming man, getting proximate to us, and being Emmanuel, God with us. That wasn't simple or easy or clean. It took sacrifice. It took time. It meant pain. But he crossed the gap.

Now he calls us to do the same.

HOW WELL DO YOU CROSS CULTURES?

How would you rate your ability to cross culture? If you want to grow in cultural competency, a healthy first step is establishing a baseline.

Here are some questions to ask yourself. Don't beat yourself up if you don't like the answers. This is a starting point. Just answer honestly:

- How many trusting relationships do I have with people who have a different economic, political, or ethnic background from me?
- Where do I spend my time? How often do I engage in environments where I am different from others? Where I might be "the only one" in the group with my background?
- Am I able to speak freely with people who are different from me, even if it is difficult for them to hear what I have to say?
- When I disagree with someone, do I move toward them or away from them?

- Can I speak with others in such a way that they are valued and respected, even when I have something to say they do not agree with?
- What music do I listen to? What books do I read? Are they from diverse artists and authors?
- How much do I educate myself on different cultures and/or different viewpoints on a particular subject?
- How well do I listen?

If you look at your world and you find that you are mostly around people who are the same as you—same education, ethnicity, neighborhood, belief system, age, economic status—I want to challenge you to take a step. Think of how Jobs for Life grew out of a small (and initially awkward) step between Pastor McCoy and Chris Magnum. Be intentional and put yourself in places where people are different from you. Read, watch, and listen to books and programs that offer different perspectives. Find opportunities to be "the other" or the "only one."

Then, watch God expand your understanding of him and help you see and experience his fullness.

SO . . . WHICH LIVES MATTER, AGAIN?

I want to end by revisiting some of those lightning rod statements from earlier in this chapter that have been a part of our cultural conversation. The goal here isn't to settle these debates definitively, but to try looking at them through the lens of cultural competency. How can we become better students of culture here?

First up: Is it OK to say, "Black lives matter"?

Yes! *Of course*, Black lives matter. And it's important to call out Black lives in particular when Black people have been singled out because of their color. In context, the statement "Black lives matter" nearly always acts as an *answer* more than a standalone *statement*. After some incident of racial violence, the question arises, "Do Black lives even matter?" It is with *this* question in the background that we can affirm, unflinchingly, "Yes, Black lives matter. The souls of Black people matter. The bodies of Black people matter. Black lives are images of God, beautiful and filled with dignity."

What about "Blue lives matter" or "Police lives matter"?

Again, yes! Certainly, police lives matter. Not only are these men and women beautiful, dignity-bearing images of their Creator, they should also be honored for the sacrifices and acts of heroism they make *each day* to protect us. I, for one, do not even want to begin imagining a world in which the lives of our law enforcement officers are treated flippantly.

So Black lives matter *and* blue lives matter. Honestly, very few people would argue with either of these claims. Where things get sticky is when they seem to compete with each other.

For instance, what do we say when a police officer shoots and kills an unarmed person of color? Is it OK to say "Blue lives matter" then?

That's tough. I'll acknowledge that some of it depends on the context. Saying "Blue lives matter" does not necessarily mean police are absolved of horrific mistakes or unjust acts. But, based on the *timing*, it's very easy for a statement like this to be taken that way. This is why saying "Blue lives matter" in the face of someone or a group of people who have been the victim of that injustice is callous and shortsighted—not because it's false, but because it's culturally unaware. Cultural competence matters.

That leads us to the next statement: "All lives matter."

Certainly we can say that all lives matter. *Everyone* is an image-bearer of God and has unique value and worth. The trouble with "All lives matter" is not that we think it is untrue (it is gloriously true!), but that the timing is often unhelpful.

For instance, the slogan "All lives matter" is often brought out in response to the statement "Black lives matter." In this context, it sounds like a rebuttal. One group is attempting to elevate the importance and plight of Black lives. To respond to that with "Well, *all* lives matter" misses the entire point. It shows a deep insensitivity and unawareness of the whole reason people want and need to highlight Black lives. Again, this isn't because "All lives matter" is false, but because it can come across as culturally unaware. Cultural competence matters.

What about people, particularly Christians, who are hesitant to say, "Black lives matter," because they believe doing so is an endorsement of the Black Lives Matter organization, with which they have valid disagreements and concerns? I'd say again, study your context. There are times when someone can endorse the sentiment of "Black lives matter" without supporting the organization. And there are times when saying it is taken as a direct endorsement of the organization. It all depends.

And then finally, "Trans lives matter." Can we say that? This can get very tricky for Christians. Historically, we have dropped the ball in knowing how to engage people who have a different perspective of sexual and gender preference or identity. Christians don't even agree among themselves.

But this much seems clear: I believe we can (and must) say, "Trans lives matter." *Every* life matters to God. Every life was handcrafted by God. Every life reflects his beautiful and creative image. Regardless of how we view sexuality, regardless of whether we may be misunderstood, we must be crystal-clear in speaking of the lives of our neighbors as valuable, precious, and beloved.

There's a lot more to say about handling issues of sexuality and gender with justice, clarity, and compassion. Just hang with me, and we'll dive *deep* into those waters in Chapter 11.

EXPECT MISTAKES

All of these examples show how complex cultural competency can be. It's often not either/or (Black Lives Matter or Blue Lives Matter), but more of a both/and (Black Lives Matter and Blue Lives Matter). But even once we realize that we're in a "both/and" world, navigating that world with integrity and compassion is challenging.

Cultural competency requires understanding context, knowing history, building trust with people, extending grace, practicing forgiveness, embracing reconciliation, and prioritizing relationship. It takes time. It's really, really *tough*. Which means that even when we're trying our best, we're going to botch it along the way.

And that's OK. Mistakes are OK. Expect them. Welcome them. Because the *bigger* mistake is choosing not to engage at all. The bigger mistake is to just keep swimming along, pretending like the water around us doesn't exist.

QUESTIONS TO CONSIDER

1. How would you describe your culture? What do you like about it? What do you not like about it?
2. What cultural divides do you encounter each day?
3. What skills and savvy do you need right now to navigate those cultural divides?
4. Where do you think you are doing well with cultural competency? What is frustrating you?

CHAPTER 9

Cultural Competency and Race

I'm curious: What is your first race memory? In other words, when did you first know there was a difference among people with different races?

Even though I grew up in a wealthy White community, I went to public schools and was around racially diverse environments starting in kindergarten. Some of my best friends were African American boys and girls. I still have pictures of them displayed on the wall in the room where I grew up.

Looking back, though, I don't remember having them over to my house. Nor do I remember going over to theirs. We just saw one another at school and developed our friendships there.

I noticed differences in the way people talked and acted but nothing that seemed unusual to me at that age.

It wasn't until I was older that I experienced deep differences.

My first race memory is, like many people's, a bit disorienting and uncomfortable.

Growing up, people rarely called me David. Instead, they called me Spick (short for my last name). Sometimes, that was just natural. Since David is a common name, people often used my last name or a shortened version of it to identify me. This nickname has been passed down from generation to generation in my family. My grandfather's friends called him Spick, my father's friends called him Spick, and my older brother's friends called him Spick.

And so, my friends called me Spick.

We all loved it. There's something about having a nickname. It gives you a feeling of uniqueness, like people really know you.

But you may be able to see where this is headed. One day, when I was in grade school, my baseball coach told me something that shocked me: Calling someone Spick is a racial slur for Hispanic populations, just like the N-word is for African-Americans.[27]

Because I had no interaction with Hispanic communities, I had no idea. It wasn't until I was in high school and in the Miami airport that I realized how problematic it was.

I was with a group from my church. We were traveling on a mission trip and had a layover in Miami. As our plane was starting to board, I was in the bathroom and members of my group were looking for me. As I exited the restroom, one of them saw me and yelled—I mean really *yelled*, "Hey, Spick! Our plane is about to board!"

You should have seen the faces of the people around us. They were appalled. They could not believe someone would use that racial slur, much less call it out in a public setting filled with Hispanic people. As we realized what had happened, we hurriedly got on the plane.

I no longer introduce myself as Spick. Most people call me David now. And no one calls my children Spick. That nickname is no longer passed down in our family.

JUST LEADERS AND CULTURAL COMPETENCE

As we saw in the last chapter, just leaders—like the *tsaddiqim*—are, by necessity, culturally competent leaders. After all, if the *tsaddiqim* are working toward justice *for the whole city*, they need to understand people from the whole city. Even in a small community, there's more than enough cultural diversity to pay attention to.

As I've argued throughout the first section of this book, paying attention is central to who just leaders need to be. They see what others do not. What we're going to explore in this next section is the way we can develop the skills and insight to cross all kinds of cultural barriers.

It's not enough to see the differences. If we want to be just leaders, we have to see differences *and* bridge them.

SO . . . WHY RACE?

There are a number of cultural barriers that just leaders need to bridge, but we're going to start with one of the most pressing—and, often, the most contentious: race.

Often, when people talk about the pursuit of justice, particularly in the United States, they end up talking about racial justice. You've probably noticed this, but why is that?

Here's the short answer: Much of the injustice that has taken place in our country has centered on the differences of race. We have a long history of racial discrimination that has led to people of color having far lower rates of positive outcomes in almost every area of our society. Consider:

- Infant deaths are 2.4 times higher among Black people than among White people.[28]
- Preterm births are 2 times higher.[29]
- Out of school suspensions? Ten times higher.[30]
- Unemployment? Twice as high.[31]
- Kids in foster care? Twice as high.[32]
- Likelihood of being searched on a routine traffic stop. Two times higher.[33]
- Chances of landing in prison? Five times higher.[34]
- Average net worth? Eight times lower. *Eight times.*[35]

Some of us just accept that as "the way things are." Some of us, candidly, don't care much about it. Some of us feel paralyzed to create any change. Some of us are ignorant of these outcomes or don't believe they are legitimate.

But some of us—and I believe you're among them—are deeply burdened by these inequities. You want to be a part of the solution.

Before we get to the solution, let's back up a bit. We need to understand the problem first.

A BRIEF HISTORY OF RACE

Many of us were raised to think of race as a natural category, as obvious to everyone as a person's eye color or their height. In reality, though, the concept of race in the United States has a specific history. It didn't always exist.

The way sociologists often talk about this is by calling race a "social construct." That simply means it's more man-made than God-ordained.

Now, to be clear, not all social constructs are bad. For instance, money is a kind of social construct. The paper in our pockets (or the numbers in our bank accounts) aren't literally wealth. They aren't pieces of gold or piles of diamonds, though you can exchange your money for these things. Money represents something, and as a society, we all agree about that meaning. That agreement (which generally operates subconsciously) is a social construct. It's useful, but it's not necessary. Societies can function with some other ways of exchanging goods.

With race, though, the history is more fraught.

Race entered our society in the late 1600s when White Europeans used themselves as the model for humanity. After Bacon's Rebellion in 1691, many European nations enjoyed a period of worldwide colonial expansion. To justify their colonial aspirations, they created a race spectrum. From that point on, the color of someone's skin was attributed to power and privilege—with White skin having the greatest power and privilege and dark skin having less or even none. The whiter the skin, the more inherent goodness a person possessed.[36]

This new understanding of race differed from what we now call "ethnicity." Our ethnicity encapsulates our culture, our language, and our nationality. In biblical terms, these are the "many tribes and tongues and nations" we see gathered around the throne in Revelation. Ethnic differences pop up all throughout Scripture, representing the beauty and diversity of God's creation. He created people in his image and gave us all different cultures and flavors to reflect him.

To see the difference between race and ethnicity, consider three questions:

- How many are there?
- Who gives the label?
- How closely aligned is it with place and language?

With ethnicity, the answers are:

- A lot!
- The people do *from within*.
- Very.

With race, the answers are:

- Just two—White and non-White (and the closer to White, the greater the value)
- One group does *from the outside*.
- Sometimes aligned, but often not.

Question	Ethnicity	Race
How many are there?	A lot	Two—White and non-White
Who gives the label?	The people do from within	One group does from the outside
How closely aligned with place and language?	Very	Sometimes aligned, but often not.

So, for instance, consider a young man from Colombia who has emigrated to the United States. His ethnic identity is Colombian. This is one of hundreds—or, more likely—thousands of ethnic identities in the world. *Colombian* is the word this man will choose to describe himself and his people. It aligns perfectly with place and language: His native Spanish and his hometown of Bogotá are both significant pieces of being Colombian.

This same man, though, if seen through a racial lens, loses a lot of this distinctiveness. There are only two broad options, and depending on his skin tone, he will probably be considered Black or Brown. That designation isn't one he would naturally choose for himself, but he will have to live with the label whether he chooses to own it or not. And being Black or Brown in the United States has no connection at all to Bogotá or the Spanish language he speaks.

What I'm trying to show here is that, while all social categories are, in a sense, human constructs, some are more fitting and accurate to God's creation. Ethnicity is a good social construct, fitting for God's creation and aligning with his revelation. It honors people, their origin, their identity. Race—specifically the Western history of this social construct—is much less fitting.

A truly just society would not, therefore, deal in categories of race as much as it deals in categories of ethnicity. But given the reality of race as the framework in the United States, it's necessary to understand the framework, its unjust history, and its unjust present consequences.

OUR HORRIFYING RACIAL HISTORY

Given the origin of race as a means to assign power and privilege to people with White skin, racism can be considered a system of advantage for those considered White and of oppression for those who are not considered White.[37]

Some people really struggle with this idea that racism is basically about

White power and there are no other forms of racism. If that's the case, people of color, by definition, cannot be racist.

This is where both the history and definition of terms are extremely important. Most of us don't think of racism as a system of White power. We think of racism as another way of talking about discrimination or bigotry. If that's the case, anyone can be racist, whether you have light skin or dark skin.

And it's true: People of every ethnic group can—and, tragically, very consistently do—discriminate against those in other groups. While racism is inherently tied to White power, discrimination and bias *can* exist in various directions among different ethnicities. This understanding of racism doesn't make all people of color immediately innocent (any more than talking about sexism means that all societal problems are inherently male); rather, this definition of racism identifies a specific *type* of bias with a very specific *history*. But understanding how the term was first developed is critical to knowing how to address it.

No matter how we define it, we cannot deny the horrifying racial history we have in our country that has oppressed Black and Brown people to the advantage of those of us who society considers White. None of us can truly comprehend the displacement experienced by indigenous peoples, the horrors they experienced as they were "re-educated" to become more like "civilized Whites." We won't truly get the brutal treatment of enslaved Africans, the physical and emotional torture they endured, and the baseless rhetoric White people used to claim that their subjugation was justified—or even, somehow, beneficial to those being enslaved.

Many of us who are White get tired of hearing about the treatment of indigenous peoples or the many years of American slavery as the cause for Black and Brown people's problems today. We might honestly believe, for instance, that pointing to slavery as the cause is a convenient excuse or is no longer relevant since it happened hundreds of years ago and has been illegal for generations. We don't realize how shortsighted we are to put the impacts of slavery (or other historical injustices) in a box and think it has no impact today.

Bryan Stevenson, author of *Just Mercy* and founder of the Equal Justice Initiative, describes how racism did not end in America; it has only evolved. Thus the only way we will heal from it is to face it, not run from it:

> We need a new era of truth and justice that starts with confronting our history of racial injustice. The dehumanizing myth of racial difference endures today because we don't talk about it.[38]

That's why he and his team created the National Museum for Peace and Justice in Montgomery, Alabama, a museum that honors victims of lynching from the Jim Crow era. Stevenson contends that you cannot go to Germany and not see memorials of victims of the Holocaust, nor can you go to Rwanda and not be faced with the brutal history of its civil war.[39] Those countries' willingness to face their own trauma, however uncomfortable, has led to real healing.

I went to the National Museum for Peace and Justice and was profoundly impacted by the displays of men and women, primarily from the South, with their names and locations of their killing. The locations are identified by county, so if you go and are from the South, you can find the names and dates of those killed by lynching in the counties where you live. You are then encouraged to take a replica of the memorial to your county and set up a monument in the location of the lynching to honor the victims so no one will forget their names and what happened to them.

This is a picture of the *imago Dei*—valuing every human being as an image-bearer of God with a step of remembering and lamenting the horror we inflicted on our fellow men and women—a powerful and necessary step toward healing.

And yet, unpeeling the onion of race in America cannot stop there. There are many more layers.

Slavery may have legally ended with the Civil War, but the narrative of racial difference that drove it did not. In many ways, it evolved through policies that continued to oppress Black and Brown people.

It evolved in the form of Jim Crow laws, which first appeared as early as the 1870s and lasted nearly a century. These laws made segregation the law of the land, limiting (or eliminating) access that Black people had to basic infrastructure—trains, restaurants, schools.

It evolved in the form of redlining, begun by the National Housing Act of 1934. When Congress passed this act, they drew up "residential security maps" of hundreds of American cities, literally labeling parts of each city by color—green, blue, yellow, and red. Lenders were told to focus on the "green" and to avoid the "red" (hence the term *redlining*). Which neighborhoods were "red"? Those with disproportionate concentrations of Black families. The result? A new closed ecosystem of poverty that was nearly impossible to break out of.

It evolved in the way the GI Bill was administered in 1944. On paper, this bill was supposed to give returning WW2 veterans low-interest housing loans. But to apply, you had to go directly to the VA officials, nearly all of whom were White. Repeatedly, Black applicants were simply turned down. In one city, of the 67,000 mortgages insured by the GI Bill, fewer than one hundred went to non-Whites.[40] As I mentioned earlier, my own family benefited from this.

It evolved in the war on drugs, which brought the hammer of punishment down disproportionately on the poor. The criminal focus on crack use, for instance, meant Black populations were repeatedly targeted. Crack, being an impure form of cocaine, is more prevalent among poorer populations, many of them people of color. But even though there are three times as many cocaine users as crack users, the penalty for crack use is *eighteen times* more stringent than for cocaine.[41]

It evolved into a culture of incarceration, where for the exact same crimes, White inmates end up in prison less often and consistently serve shorter sentences once there. For a male prisoner, under twenty-five, with no prior offenses, 30 percent of Whites are granted parole, but only 14 percent of Blacks or Latinos are.[42]

It evolved into our present-day reality, in which police brutality still plagues our cities.

NINE MINUTES AND TWENTY-NINE SECONDS

I was sitting on my porch when my daughter came in and said another Black man had been killed by a White police officer. I didn't think much of it because sadly these events had become far too common. Armaud Arbery, the young man who was shot and killed in Georgia while jogging, had been dominating the news and conversations I was having with friends and family. I did not think an incident could overshadow that.

But then I started to see news reports about the latest killing. It was in Minnesota, and the man was George Floyd. It was late at night, and I saw there was a link I could click to watch the footage. People said it was gruesome. I was scared to watch it then as I knew it would keep me up, so I waited until the morning.

Shock, horror, disbelief—I was speechless after I clicked on the link the next morning.

Nine minutes and twenty-nine seconds, according to the prosecutor: the time the police officer held George Floyd down with his knee on Mr. Floyd's neck.

To me, it looked like a modern-day lynching.

On the one hand, I found solidarity with my friends of color who felt the same way. They were horrified and terrified. Absolutely petrified for themselves—and particularly for their sons.

At the same time, my shock also fell on deaf ears. It was as if some of my friends were saying to me, "David, why are you so surprised? This has been happening to us for years, decades, even centuries. Where have you been?"

As a White person, particularly a White male, when it comes to race, it is easy to feel deep guilt and shame. Sometimes, I even wish I wasn't White.

I struggle with the idea that people seem to hold people like me responsible when we weren't the ones who promoted slavery. *We didn't live during Jim Crow. We value all people. Why are we the problem?*

Many of my White friends have shut down in the face of these ideas and don't want any part of these conversations. *Don't tell me I'm a racist. Don't put the blame on me.*

But as Christians, as those who follow the God of justice who has justified us all not because of what we have done, but because of what Jesus has done for us, shouldn't we welcome these conversations? Shouldn't we be the first in line to look at the speck in our own eye rather than the log in others' eyes?

WHAT DOES THIS MEAN FOR THE WORKPLACE?

At this point, you may be asking, "What does all of this mean for my scope of leadership? For my organization, my people, my workplace? How can I create an environment of belonging where people feel comfortable expressing their God-given ethnicity and culture?"

I'm not naive enough to think I can solve racism with some quick and easy applications. You aren't, either. But there are some basic ways we can begin to apply this, even starting today. Four key areas come to mind:

1. Focus on your posture. No, not your literal posture. Your posture toward the entire race conversation. As we saw in the first part of this book, it's important for us to begin with the question, "What do I see?" If you are curious to learn about your blind spots, seeing more of yourself and others in the process, your posture will naturally change—from a bracing posture of defensiveness to an open posture of humility and empathy.

One CEO I work with put it well: "The best posture I can have is a vulnerable one. The first thing I have to say is, 'I have a lot to learn.'"

2. Learn about your leadership context. In one way or another, racism has impacted your specific field. Perhaps you already know some of that history. Perhaps not. Either way, asking a few questions will quickly highlight how much more there is to learn. Don't shy away from this: The more you understand the history that has led to fractured racial issues, the better poised you'll be to create a counterculture of flourishing.

You'll have to do this, not just with your field, but with your specific organization, too. Ask tough, introspective questions: *What has prevented us from being diverse? Why have we been content with this lack of diversity?* Knowing where you've come from will help you know where to go next.

3. Link DEI (Diversity, Equity, and Inclusion) initiatives to your mission, vision, and strategic plan. Many leaders begin to make moves to address racism, but those initiatives live on an island. But rather than having a separate DEI plan, you should look for ways to integrate justice into your current strategic plan. Lead the way by championing DEI initiatives from the top, then ensure that they get worked out in strategic ways throughout your entire organization.

4. Remember that the ultimate goal is to not to check a box, but to create a just organization. The goal here is not a specific diversity benchmark. The goal here is justice, which means that a company need not be ethnically diverse to be just. What matters more than diverse representation is whether a leader is acting as an agent of healing change in their industry, addressing real issues faced by people of color, and encouraging their organization to do so, too. Of course, an all-White organization will have to work very hard to stay close to people of color in other meaningful ways—through learning, or strategic partnerships, or friendships. Often, diversity will be the by-product of just practices. But it's important that we keep the cart and horse in the right order—justice first, diversity as a result.

Solving the issues of racial justice in the United States is tremendously complicated. I'm not suggesting that one book—or one chapter—can do it. But if we Christians want to be people of justice in the midst of our cities, we must be ready to see injustice in all its ugliness—in our cities, in our neighborhoods, even in ourselves.

By God's grace, we can do so from a place of both repentance and freedom. Every punishment for racism and bigotry and discrimination has already been taken care of. Jesus paid it all. We can walk now without defensiveness. With justice.

QUESTIONS TO CONSIDER

1. What's your first memory of race?
2. What keeps you from engaging those who are racially or ethnically different from you?
3. What compels you to get close to those who are racially or ethnically different from you?
4. Who do you need to learn from to become more culturally competent in your leadership?

CHAPTER 10

Cultural Competency and Poverty

If we want to be just leaders who engage in *mishpat*, we must have an understanding of poverty and how to engage those in need. Remember the "quartet of the vulnerable"—the orphans, widows, immigrants, and the poor? Just leaders are those who engage these groups in ways that lead them from despair to hope, from floundering to flourishing—and find that the more they lead others to thrive, the more they themselves thrive.

So, what does it look like to be leaders who effectively cross socioeconomic lines and build meaningful connections with those in material need? How can we bring joy to those in poverty?

Poverty is pervasive, both in the United States and across the world. As of this writing, there are over 38 million people in the United States who live in poverty, the highest amount in our country's history. And almost half the world—3.4 billion people—live on less than $5.50 per day.[43]

In the United States, the poverty rate (the percentage of the overall population living in poverty) has remained between 10 and 15 percent of the population since 1965. Across the world, one billion children live in poverty (that's one in two children worldwide), and 356 million live in extreme poverty.[44]

People are considered poor in the United States if they earn less than what's outlined in the federal government's official poverty thresholds. In 2023, the threshold for a family of four was $27,750, or $2,313 per month.[45] That means that if you make $27,750 or less, you are legally considered one of the 38 million poor people in the United States. If you make just one dollar more, $27,751, you are not poor. Not legally, anyway.

Except that, in another real sense, you still are. Can you imagine trying to provide for a family of four with only $27,751? Even $30,000 or $40,000 would pose a significant challenge. That's why when people look at these statistics—which are already rather jarring—they know they only tell part of the story.[46] Many more than 38 million people in our nation are struggling with poverty.

Another way to think about income and poverty is provided by the Economic Policy Institute. This group has created the Family Budget Calculator to measure the income a family needs in order to attain a modest yet adequate standard of living. The budgets estimate community-specific costs for ten family types (one or two adults with zero to four children) in all counties and metro areas in the United States. Compared with the federal poverty line and the Supplemental Poverty Measure, EPI's family budgets provide a more accurate and complete measure of economic security in America.

I entered my city, Raleigh, North Carolina, and basic family information (two adults, two children) and the calculator said to attain a modest standard of living, I would need an income of $7,487/month (or $89,845 a year). Expenses include housing, food, childcare, transportation, healthcare, taxes, and a handful of others.

(Remember that $27,750/year poverty line? A modest standard of living towers over that number by a factor of three.)

For New York City, the number is $11,245 per month, or $134,938 a year.

In the poorest county in Kentucky (Owsley), the amount is $5,647 per month[47]—$67,768 a year.

Millions and millions of people, many more than the number identified in poverty, struggle to take care of themselves and their families. They include those working at minimum wage (often holding down several jobs), seniors living on fixed incomes who can't afford their medicine, those in the military, young adults, and wage earners who are suddenly out of work. They live in big cities and rural communities. The faces of poverty are incredibly varied—and devastatingly vast.

With little hope, people sink deeper and deeper, physically and emotionally, into a hole they cannot escape.

So, what do we do? How do we engage?

ASK THE RIGHT QUESTIONS

I've worked at the intersection of plenty and poverty for much of my career. In my experience, people ask a handful of the same questions when they consider engaging people in need. Some of these are helpful; others, less so. Here are some of the most common:

- How do I get over my fears of engaging people in need?
- Should I feel guilty about the resources and wealth I have?
- Should I give money to the person on the side of the road?
- If Jesus says, "The poor you will always have with you," why should I even try to end poverty?
- Why are people poor? Is it a result of choices they have made or broken systems around them?
- How does poverty relate to issues like unemployment, health, education, race, gentrification, affordable housing, or incarceration?
- What terms should we use when describing people in poverty?

Like I said, many of these questions are helpful. But as you consider these questions, I want to ask a couple more:

- What part of your story **keeps you** from engaging the material poor?
- What part of your story **compels you** to engage the material poor?

As I have said before, I grew up with a real desire to engage people in need. I don't know where that came from. I lived in a big home in a nice part of the city. I went to a private high school. I was often around people with means.

There wasn't a particular experience I can point to which gave me that desire. I went on mission trips when I was in high school that allowed me to see poverty up close and appreciate what I have, but the desire to be near people in need came even before going on these trips. I certainly felt compelled because of what I read about Jesus and what he did when he came to earth. But there was something more—a gravitation to things that are hard, where there is struggle and grit, and a need to depend on one another and on God. A desire to be around people different from me, to see and experience other cultures, and to have a deeper understanding of what's going on around me. I did not want to stay in my safe, somewhat easy, and even boring world. I felt that engaging people in need put me on the front lines, dealing with *real* issues. I wanted to push myself to rely less on what I have and more on others and God.

That doesn't mean this is easy for me or that I am some saint. Quite the opposite. In fact, if people looked at my life *right now*, they might say, "David, where are the places where you are engaging people in need right now?" And I would say, "Not many." I have the usual excuses that keep me from taking those steps—I don't have enough time, I want to remain comfortable, I don't want to put myself in a position where I need to be seen as the solution to someone else's problems, I don't want to be interrupted, I don't know if I will need to give up my money to help . . . and that's just what I could come up with off the top of my head!

So, don't be afraid of asking the tough questions about your motivations. They're tough for me, too. But with this issue, as in so many others, the tough questions are the right ones.

YOU (YES, YOU) ARE POOR, TOO

When surveying a group of well-resourced leaders in my community, these were the biggest obstacles they identified for not engaging someone in need:

- I don't know what to do (62 percent)
- I don't have time (55 percent)
- I'm nervous about doing it wrong (34 percent)
- I don't think about it (14 percent)
- I don't know anyone who is poor (7 percent)

After hearing their answers, the group was asked a different question: What do the materially poor have that you wish you had? Here were the answers:

- desperation
- deep dependency on God
- simplicity
- community
- freedom from performance
- humility
- relationships
- less worry about possessions
- reliance on others
- vulnerability
- willingness to take risks
- joy in all circumstances

I find these answers interesting for two reasons. First, note the perception of what we believe those living in poverty have. We assume the above list is what those in poverty experience. In many cases, these qualities are true of people in need, but they aren't automatic results of poverty. Many people struggling in poverty would *also* like to have the things we assume they have!

Second, and more importantly, since this is what people *perceive* for those in need, *these answers reveal our own poverty.* They reveal the things we wish we had—but don't. Like the ways in which we rely on our own strength rather than on God, or how we are prone to anxiety, depression, and love of our possessions. They reveal how we worry about not having enough, how we lack vulnerability, how we feel isolated from relationships, how we struggle with pride and envy, how we lack joy.

Whether our perception of poverty is right or not, it's vital to recognize our own poverty. In fact, that's the first step to engage people in material need: Recognize that you, too, are poor. You are needy. You are lacking something. Upon that common ground, we can begin to build something beautiful as we reach out to those who are hurting.

Unless we begin by understanding our own poverty, our efforts will not have the effect we want. As Brian Fikkert and Steve Corbett note in their book *When Helping Hurts*, "Until we embrace our mutual brokenness, our work with low-income people is likely to do more harm than good."[48]

If we approach people as if we have something they need and we can fix them (You may not say it, but if you're honest, you've thought it. I have, too!), we can unintentionally reduce poor people to objects we use to fulfill our own needs. But when we understand our *mutual* brokenness, we instead can enter into a meaningful relationship.

In other words, we should be able to identify with poor people. It's similar to the way God views poor people. God does not just care for poor people; he identifies with them. As Jesus said, "As you did it to one of the least of these my brothers, you did it to me" (Matthew 25:40). Pastor Tim Keller, reflecting on this verse, writes, "If a person doesn't care about the poor, it reveals that at best he doesn't understand the grace he has experienced, and at worst he has not really encountered the saving mercy of God."[49]

Our proximity to poor people, therefore, puts us close to God. We've already talked about this as to why serving people in need is not optional. It's a true mark of being a follower of Jesus. It's a question of whether the love of God is in us (see 1 John 3:17).

And so we pursue people in need, not because of *their* brokenness, but because of *our shared* brokenness—and our common need for God and one another. Separated from one another, none of us are on the road to thriving. Together, we can learn to flourish.

WRONG MOTIVATIONS to engage those in need	**RIGHT MOTIVATIONS to engage**
Trying to fix them	Seeing their unique dignity and value
Making them more like us	Listening to and learning from them
Earning God's favor	Experiencing the fullness of God
Feeling guilty for what we have	Being grateful for what we have and using all of it to advance God's Kingdom

WRONG MOTIVATIONS *not* to engage those in need	**RIGHT MOTIVATIONS to engage**
Not knowing what to do	Wanting to know their name
Not being able to relate to them or their story	Finding something we may have in common and building a relationship with them
Not having enough time	Discovering ways to engage those in need in everything we do
Assuming they have nothing to offer	Recognizing they have so much to offer

SO . . . WHAT, EXACTLY, IS POVERTY?

Once we begin to see ourselves in the right light, we can begin to think rightly about poverty. Most of us have a definition of poverty, but few of us have picked up the definition with any intentionality. Chances are, if I were to ask you, you would define poverty as a lack of material possessions.

But is that the most fundamental element of poverty? Or is it something deeper? Quoting Fikkert and Corbett again:

Poverty is the result of relationships that do not work, that are not just, that are not for life, that are not harmonious or enjoyable. Poverty is the absence of *shalom* in all its meanings.[50]

Fikkert and Corbett argue that poverty is less about material lack and more about broken relationships. After all, if poverty were primarily a lack of material goods, all we would have to do is give people what they do not have and poverty would be solved. But we all know poverty is much more complex than that. They go on to say:

While poor people mention having a lack of material things, they tend to describe their condition in far more psychological and social terms than our North American audiences. Poor people typically talk in terms of shame, inferiority, powerlessness, humiliation, fear, hopelessness, depression, social isolation, and voicelessness. North American audiences tend to emphasize a lack of material things such as food, money, clean water, medicine, housing, etc.[51]

The goal of engaging with those in poverty, therefore, is not to make sure that the material poor have enough money. (That may be part of what we do, but it is not the center.) Rather, the goal is to restore people to a full expression of humanness. To restore *shalom*. To multiply justice and joy in the city. To help our neighbors thrive.

SO . . . HOW DO WE ENGAGE?

All of this raises the question you've been asking all chapter: *How* do we engage people in poverty?

As with many issues of justice, we often want a pattern to follow—a formula of rights and wrongs to know we're on track. But we're talking about *loving people*, and that's a messy business. People are complicated. Love is complicated. So, when we consider our plan of action, it's important to remember that (as I pointed out in the last chapter) our *posture* toward those in need often matters more than any particular *action*.

If I were to sum up my advice for poverty work in one (maddeningly subjective) word, it would be *dignity*. Ask yourself what it would look like to affirm the dignity of the person in front of you. How could you speak value into their lives? How could you elevate them? How could you make them feel the inherent worth they have as a person made in the very image of God?

These aren't simple questions with simple answers. But I have found that the more I think in terms of dignity (and the less I think in terms of problems and solutions), the closer I get to the pattern of Jesus.

One tangible way this manifests is in the words we choose. Our words matter. For instance, I don't mind someone calling me a North Carolinian. I love being part of the Tar Heel State. But it would really bother me if someone decided to label me a "Confederate." Technically, North Carolina was part of the Confederacy, but that's not a connotation I want.

So it is with those who are struggling. We need to be careful to speak with words and terms that uplift and elevate the value and dignity of those in need.

Here are a few simple ways we can swap out some of our unhelpful terms for more gracious terms, those marked by dignity. As you read this list, ask yourself if there are some terms for the material poor you need to start or stop using.

Unhelpful Terms	Dignity Terms
The homeless	Man or woman who is homeless
The poor	People in material need
Ex-con, felon	Previously incarcerated man or woman
Third world	Majority world
Them/those people	Us, we, our
Least of these	Neighbor

We can—and should!—also integrate a poverty focus into our businesses. I'll get more into the nuts and bolts of this in Quality 4 ("Take Bold, Courageous Action"), but it's worth mentioning in brief here: Many Christians limit their engagement with poverty to their personal lives (which is great), but leaders have unique opportunities to become agents of thriving at a community level. Your company can help to transform the fractured community around you into a flourishing one.

One hospital CEO captured this community focus well. At a meeting with his senior executives, he said, "This is my vision for this hospital: We will become a blessing to this city. I want to see the people of this city flourish because this hospital exists."[52]

Do you have this kind of vision for your company? I'm sure you have big goals, but if your definition of success doesn't extend outward to impact the community in which you operate, I'd say your vision needs to be bigger. It should be big enough to serve your city in a way that makes even the poorest of the poor rejoice.

In our work with business leaders, we've compiled a list of the qualities of a just company. It's nowhere near exhaustive, but it's a helpful exercise to get business leaders thinking about how to engage poverty *as a leader*, not just as an individual. Here are a few examples:

- Just companies know the history of their community—and what has led to injustice.
- Just companies pay livable wages.
- Just companies "leave some on the edges," pursuing opportunities for modern-day gleaning.
- Just companies get (and stay) proximate to people in need.
- Just companies provide access to those who do not have access.
- Just companies expand their networks beyond what's normal and comfortable.
- Just companies root themselves in a specific place, committing to the flourishing of their geographical community.
- Just companies are extravagantly generous with their time and money.

JOY'S COMPLICATED STORY

More than anything, we must recognize the complexity of poverty. One of the best questions people bring to the issue of poverty was one I mentioned earlier in this chapter: *How does poverty relate to issues like unemployment, health, education, race, gentrification, affordable housing, or incarceration?*

The reality is that poverty doesn't exist in a vacuum. It is a complex—and tragic—reality. I learned this in a heartbreaking way when I met Joy and heard her story.

Joy grew up with her single mom and siblings. Her mom got by on public assistance, and her dad was nowhere to be found. Child support from her dad was never a possibility, so Joy, her mom, and her siblings lived from one disbursement check to another, not receiving anywhere close to what they needed to get by. It didn't help that her mom had a drinking problem. Any money they had funded her addiction and kept her away from the home day and night.

Joy's "job," therefore, was to run over to her grandparents' home to ask them for help. Whenever there was a need for food or a bill to be paid, which was often, her mom would give her the word and she'd head that way.

At first, doing this seemed innocent enough to Joy. After all, she was their first grandchild, and her grandparents loved her so much. Asking for their help was easy to do. With the absence of Joy's mom, she had grown close to her grandmother and loved spending time with her.

Upon arriving at her grandparents' home the first time, her grandmother told her to go ask her grandfather as he was the one who controlled the money. She had a side cleaning job, but her husband had a vibrant bootlegging business. Undercover, he had built a growing customer base, sourcing his booze from various dealers and reselling it for a profit. It turns out he was pretty good at it.

Joy wasn't very aware of the details of what he did but was just glad he'd be willing to assist them. When she arrived and approached her grandfather, he was happy to help. There was just one catch. Joy needed to do "something" for him.

"Don't tell your grandmother," Joy's grandfather said to her. "It would kill her." Confused and afraid, Joy kept quiet. She didn't want to do anything that would hurt her grandmother. So she walked out of her grandfather's room, money in hand, and quietly made her way back home.

Her mind was rushing. Thoughts of what had just happened and what her grandfather had said coursed through her mind. "In order for me to help you, you need to let me do this," he had said. What was she to do? No one had ever touched her in those places. It made her feel dirty and alone. But how else was she going to get what her family needed? She'd never seen her grandfather act that way. He was mean, cold, frightening. Was that what it meant to be loved?

This was just the beginning. Her mom constantly needed help, so Joy frequently had to go see her grandfather. She'd go out of obedience, knowing what she'd have to do to receive her grandfather's "help." He molested her every time; the pattern never stopped. And it became the defining experience of every male interaction Joy had growing up—male cousins, uncles, and other men in the community. All of them "touched on" her.

Joy hated men, but she also knew she had something they wanted. That led her to prostitution and drugs. She was good at letting men touch her while becoming callous to its effects on her. It wasn't until she was paired with a drug dealer that she experimented with drugs. He convinced her to take a drug so he could do what he wanted with her and she wouldn't have to feel it. When she took the drug, she felt something she hadn't felt before. Her pain drifted away, and she could escape from all that was happening to her.

For twenty years, this was her life. During that time, she had six children—three boys and three girls—with five different fathers. Every time one of her children was born, her mother and sister were in the delivery room, and social workers put the kids into the care of the state. That gave Joy the freedom to carry on her lifestyle.

She got so tired of the street that she started dealing drugs. That made her feel like she was helping. Women would flock to her, and she'd take care of them by helping them get high. After a while, she realized she wasn't really helping them. She was only hurting them.

And then, one day, the police raided her home.

Later, Joy said that was the best day of her life. Why? Because as she said, she was "sick and tired of being sick and tired." God used the time in prison for Joy to get ahold of herself and understand who she really was. She was aided by a group of women who came faithfully to the prison to build friendships with the women inside and talk about Jesus. One in particular, Margie, developed a deep relationship with Joy. The two of them hit it off and truly became sisters.

Joy was released from prison, found a full-time job and was able to secure housing for herself and her children. Today, Joy and Margie cannot imagine life without each other. They are lifelong friends and can't remember a time when they weren't a significant part of each other's lives. Joy is fully able to experience . . . joy.

Joy's experience of poverty was as complicated as it was brutal. We see others outside of her contributing to her terrible plight. We see Joy herself, feeling powerless and hopeless, making decisions that don't help the situation. We see an ecosystem around Joy that offers "ways out," all of which amplify the damaging effects of her poverty.

There isn't a single, simple solution to a story like Joy's. It's complicated. It's messy. It's painful.

But it's not hopeless.

HE BECAME POOR FOR US

In the Gospel of Luke, Jesus tells a parable about a man who cared for a stranger who was in desperate need:

> But a Samaritan, as he journeyed, came to where he was, and when he saw him, he had compassion. He went to him and bound up his wounds, pouring on oil and wine. Then he set him on his own animal and brought him to an inn and took care of him. And the next day he took out two denarii and gave them to the innkeeper, saying, "Take care of him, and whatever more you spend, I will repay you when I come back." (Luke 10:33–35)

Consider this Samaritan man. He had compassion on the stranger. He was proactive and prepared to help. He touched the man, even though it made him ritually unclean. He crossed a cultural boundary. He took an incredible risk, pausing to care for someone who had just been beaten (were the attackers still nearby?). He took on the nature of a servant. He leveraged his relationships for the sake of the stranger. He gave money—and promised to give more.

And then, consider Jesus, "our Samaritan," the one who became poor for us. Jesus had compassion on us when we were estranged from God. He was proactive and prepared to help, offering his very Spirit to bring us new life. He touched us in our darkest and most painful moments, even though it would eventually lead to his death. He crossed the cultural boundary between heaven and earth to be near us. He took an incredible risk, not merely caring for us in our brokenness, but being broken on the cross for our sakes. He took on the nature of a servant, loving those who would soon murder him. He leveraged all that he had for our sakes. And he gave not merely money, but something more valuable—his very life—so we could experience peace and wholeness.

Jesus, our "Samaritan," provides the model for engaging the messy world of poverty. As business leaders, we have tremendous opportunities to partner with people in poverty. People with plenty and people with little—justice nudges us toward one another, then propels us down the road to thriving.

Together.

QUESTIONS TO CONSIDER

1. What keeps you from engaging those who are materially poor?
2. What wrong motivations for engaging those in material need do you need to change?
3. How might your leadership help everyone win, particularly those who are materially poor?
4. How can you still impact those in need from a distance?

CHAPTER 11

Cultural Competency and Sexuality and Gender

On June 4, 2022, the Tampa Bay Rays held their Pride Night promotion. Part of this promotion included wearing uniforms with modified logos. Traditionally, the logo on the Rays' cap is a white "TB" with simple gold starburst shoulder patches on the jerseys. For the promotion, the Rays wore variations on both logos, adding rainbow colors, a pattern that has symbolized gay rights and support for LGBTQ+ people.

But not everyone sported the rainbow-adorned gear that night. Five of the Tampa Bay pitchers wore their standard uniforms instead.

Jason Adam, one of the pitchers, explained their reasoning:

So it's a hard decision. Because ultimately we all said what we want is them to know that all are welcome and loved here. But when we put it on our bodies, I think a lot of guys decided that it's just a lifestyle that maybe—not that they look down on anybody or think differently—it's just that maybe we don't want to encourage it if we believe in Jesus, who's encouraged us to live a lifestyle that would abstain from that behavior, just like [Jesus] encourages me as a heterosexual male to abstain from sex outside of the confines of marriage. It's no different.

Manager Kevin Cash said the players' decision didn't create any division in the clubhouse. Everyone was given the option to wear the pride caps and patches—and most did—but no one was required to.

Cash said, "I think what it has created is, like, what you've heard—a lot of conversation and valuing the different perspectives inside the clubhouse but really appreciating the community that we're trying to support here."[53]

When it comes to the reactions in the clubhouse, we'll have to take Cash's word for it. Maybe it really was as positive as he describes. But we don't have to speculate about reactions *outside* the clubhouse.

The public response to the event was vocal, widespread, and passionate. On one side, many praised the dissenting players, calling them heroes for their courage. They were considered the noble few, standing up for truth even though it was unpopular.

On the other side, the critiques poured in. These men weren't heroes, but bigots. They were judging LGBTQ+ people and demonstrating a total lack of love. Not only was that antithetical to their faith—aren't Christians people of love?—but more importantly, it was horribly intolerant. We've moved beyond this as a society, the critics claimed. Intolerance like that has no place here anymore. If you love someone, you affirm them. Either that or you are hatefully judging them. You can't have it both ways.

Perhaps you followed this whole conversation when it happened. Or perhaps this is new to you. Either way, it's helpful to ask, *How would you have acted in that situation?* What if you were the player sporting the rainbow who had to take the field with a teammate that abstained? What if you were one of the pitchers that felt uncomfortable with the Pride Night promotion? What about the manager, who knew he had very different people in his dugout? Or the PR specialist, feeling pressure from opposing sides urging the organization to "take a stand"?

If you're anything like me, even as simple a situation as this begins to feel difficult to navigate. Honestly, I'm not quite sure what I would have done in each of those roles. Odds are, regardless of your convictions here, you feel about as disoriented as me. You probably feel, as I do, *torn*. And not just about the Rays. About your organization.

You want to be inclusive, but you don't want "inclusivity" to alienate people in your organization (or your potential customers).

You want to follow the pattern of Scripture, but you also know that Christians have disagreed on these issues and may have been cruel toward those in the gay community.

You want to be loving toward those in the LGBTQ+ community, but you don't know how to show love when you may not agree with the LGBTQ+ lifestyle.

You want to cultivate a welcoming work environment for all people, but you honestly don't know where the gender conversation will go next—which may scare you.

You feel torn.

As leaders, we're doing our best to follow Jesus, making our businesses places of equity, justice, and flourishing. We want everyone around us to *thrive.*

So when it comes to sexuality and gender, what in the world does that mean? Or, to put a bit more of a point on it: *How do we, as leaders, approach gender and sexuality well, knowing that the people we are leading have strong and (often) contradictory convictions?*

GENDER AND SEXUALITY: A FEW FOUNDATIONAL PRINCIPLES

I want to be crystal clear on this: My purpose for this chapter isn't to convince you of what is right or wrong about sexual preference or gender identity. That's not because I don't care or the Bible is irrelevant on the topic. It's extremely relevant. But this isn't the place for that discussion. If you're looking to learn about a biblical approach to sexuality and gender, you'd do well to check out some of the many helpful resources out there.[54]

As I mentioned earlier, Christians don't agree with one another on how to engage people with different understandings of sexual preference and gender identity. (For that matter, neither do non-Christians!) And no matter how big of a team you lead, it's a near guarantee that people will bring drastically different views to the table. So it can be very difficult to navigate these issues well as a leader.

For many of you, the tendency may be to avoid and ignore. Just keep your head down and hope you don't end up in some kind of Tampa Bay Rays situation. I understand the impulse. And honestly, that might have worked (sorta) a few years ago. But it's becoming an increasingly impossible approach. Plus, deep down, most of us sense that can't be right. In what other area of leadership is it best to simply *ignore* something because it's complicated? No, good leaders lean in, especially when things get complicated.

Given the nature of the issue, I'm guessing readers of this book will come from a variety of perspectives.

You may be convinced that the Bible teaches that God has designed marriage to be a covenant between one man and one woman, for life. Or you may be convinced that the LGBTQ+ lifestyle is a faithful way to honor the Bible's teaching.

You may believe that God created two distinct genders, male and female—that gender is given, not chosen. Or you may be open to more gender fluid expressions.

Issues of sexuality and gender may be of first importance to you, something you think about daily. Or they may be issues that rarely cross your mind.

Wherever you land, you need to be equipped to address the question I posed earlier: how do we approach gender and sexuality well, knowing that the people we are leading have strong and (often) contradictory convictions?

Let's go back to the Tampa Bay Rays again for a moment. Consider a few more questions:

- Is it possible to disagree with the LGBTQ+ lifestyle yet still wear a uniform with rainbow colored logos to show your value of LGBTQ+ people? Or does doing so convey something you do not support?

- Did the Rays pitchers do the right thing by not wearing the uniforms with the rainbow-colored logos? How about in the way they described their decision later?
- Is it possible to disagree with the players who chose not to wear the rainbow uniform and still respect them?
- What does Christlike love look like in a context like this? Can you love someone and accept them while choosing not to affirm their behavior and lifestyle? Or is that hypocritical?
- If you have convictions about someone's sexual or gender choices, are you therefore automatically judging their identity, too?

These questions aren't just specific to the Tampa Bay example. Many of us have encountered situations—in our workplace, in our friendships, and in our interactions with family members—that raise similar questions.

In order to be more loving and accepting, some Christians today believe we need to revise our beliefs. And certainly, it's worth asking ourselves whether our beliefs truly are arising from the Bible's teaching. The Bible doesn't miss, but sometimes when we read it, we do.

However, I don't believe the only way forward is to change our beliefs. Instead, our challenge is to hold to our convictions without using those convictions to condemn or push people away.

So, what does justice and cultural competency look like *here*?

SEVEN PRINCIPLES THAT SHOULD GUIDE US

There is no easy grid to help us navigate all the landmines we may face in conversations about gender and sexuality, but there are some core principles that can guide us. These don't make the questions we mentioned earlier magically simple, but they provide us with a biblical lens of justice and wisdom. They give us a bit more confidence to navigate some otherwise choppy waters.

1. Remember that all people are made in God's image. This should be old news by this point in the book, but it's worth repeating. Since all people are made in the *imago Dei*, all people matter. Many in the LGBTQ+ community feel like society has told them they are "less than." As Christians, we can speak a clear voice to the contrary: Every LGBTQ+ person is clothed in dignity and infinite value.

2. Love like Jesus—not in affirmation or agreement, but with grace and truth. When it comes to sexuality, our society seems to have embraced a dichotomy between disagreement and acceptance. If you agree with me, you love and accept me. If you disagree with me, you don't love or accept me. There doesn't seem to be a category for accepting a person but disagreeing with them at the same time.

The Bible provides a different approach. The apostle John said that Jesus, the embodiment of love, came "full of grace and truth," not "full of agreement and affirmation." Jesus loved us more than anyone else ever could, but his love was gritty and real. He told people they were wrong. He made sacrifices for them. In other words, he spoke the truth, but he did so with grace.

Truth without grace comes across as judgment. In response, many of us think we have to show grace without any truth. But that's not helpful, either. The way forward, though it's a tough one, is the way of Jesus—truth *and* grace. We need to prove to the world that it is possible to disagree with someone *and* love them, to speak a hard truth *and* invite someone into a closer relationship with us.

I find this dynamic particularly evident with my children. If you are a parent, you know what I mean. I may disagree with my kids. I may have to have hard conversations with them. But my love for them never wavers. I'd do anything for them. Even die for them.

Achieving this, however, can be extremely difficult when there is disagreement with LGBTQ+ people concerning their lifestyle. Disagreeing with their behavior and choices can be seen rather as a judgment on their identity—who they are versus what they do. Finding common ground and building trust then can be especially challenging.

But I believe love and disagreement can happen at the same time—if there is a foundation of trust. That happens over time, in small settings, in deep relationships.

3. Honor and respect authority. Put this in the category of "We shouldn't have to say it, but we still do." Whatever you believe about sexuality, you need to follow the law. Discriminating against people based on their sexuality is illegal, and we need to do our homework to know precisely what that means for our context. Once we know it, we need to abide by it.

For instance, in the United States, marriage is legal for homosexual couples. This means that work benefits offered to heterosexual married couples (e.g., a healthcare plan) must also be made available to gay married couples. When applicable, we also need to abide by Title VII of the Civil Rights Act, which identifies specific "protected people groups," including gay, lesbian, and transgender individuals. Our hiring practices and workplace environment must be in accordance with the law.

Obeying the law isn't all that goes into loving. It's the floor, not the ceiling here. It's the least we can do. But those who follow Jesus never look to do the least work possible.

4. Prioritize your people . . . One CEO came to me concerned because their employees, particularly their homosexual employees, complained that the company did not post anything online during Pride Month affirming the LGBTQ+ community. Based on the leader's beliefs about sexuality and gender, he didn't feel it was appropriate to make a post, but he and the rest of his leadership wanted to make sure they clearly communicated value to their LGBTQ+ employees.

This situation raises questions for me, much like that of the Rays' pitchers. Does making a post communicate the value the LGBTQ+ employees desire? Is there something else that would accomplish this goal?

Would it be possible for the company to be so intentional about showing value to all of their employees that their employees wouldn't even need to have them make a public post, because they already know how valuable they are?

In a situation like this, I would encourage this CEO (and others like him) to think more about what speaks value to his people and less about what makes a *public statement*. Sure, the easiest thing to do might be to post something about Pride Month. But in addition to running against the CEO's convictions, this also may not be that meaningful to his LGBTQ+ employees! If we are seeking to promote justice in our spheres of influence, we should think more about what impacts our people than what others on the outside might think.

5. . . . But expect harsh pushback. The flip side of prioritizing your people is the unpleasant reality that *other people will be watching*. I stand by what I said: You should prioritize your people. But you also need to be ready for harsh pushback, both from inside and outside your organization. The Rays' manager tried to navigate this by focusing on the clubhouse, then later making his reasoning known to the world. But it's not surprising that the response was fractured and often angry. That's the temperature of this conversation right now.

I'm not saying we should just blast our views out there with a careless attitude. We need to speak with *grace* and *gentleness*. But as leaders, we need to be honest with ourselves and with our teams about the difficulties ahead. Even if we navigate these conversations better than most, we should expect fierce criticism from many. We simply need to see it coming and see it through.

6. Lean in. Given the volatile nature of these conversations, many of us will be tempted to shy away from them. We know how costly it can be to do or say the wrong thing. So we might want to play it safe, keep our heads down, and just hope it all goes away. That's an understandable desire. But it's not what bold leaders do. It's not what justice looks like. And it's not how we move our people toward thriving.

We are going to make some mistakes along the way. What I'm encouraging us to do is to make mistakes in the direction of relationship rather than in the direction of isolation. If you're worried about hurting someone's feelings with a public decision, reach out to them first. If you aren't sure of the best way to speak about people in the LGBTQ+ community, ask. You don't have to agree with someone to build a relationship with them. So, lean into the relationship.

This won't be a seamless or easy process. Relationships are messy. But they're also the surest way to cultivate empathy, which is what we're after. When you get to know someone, you start to wince when they might wince. You start to hear things the way they might hear them. Is that disorienting? Yes. Is it worth it? Also yes.

Knowing people on a relational, one-on-one, at-your-kitchen-table level is what allows us to love people while still disagreeing with them. Disagreement from a distance feels like judgment. But disagreement in the context of safety and acceptance and proximity? That lands differently.

We can't always control whether people call us hateful bigots or not. But we absolutely can control whether we extend a hand of love and welcome to others.

7. **Learn when to speak and when to be silent.** If you're looking for an opportunity to speak to some recent issue of gender or sexuality, you'll find one. The question is, how often should you speak to those issues? Or, to put it differently, do Christians always need to make their sexual ethic known?

The answer here depends on the context. A helpful question to ask yourself is, "Which side of the 'grace and truth' spectrum do I land on?" For those of us inclined to always speak truth, we would do well to listen more and speak less. For those of us inclined to avoid truth and only rely on grace, we need the reminder to have the courage to be honest about our convictions . . . when it's appropriate.

I can't tell you when, specifically, you have to make your convictions known and when it is kinder to simply have them unspoken. But it should probably involve a good combination of speaking *and* listening. In relationships of deep trust and proximity, you honor the other person by sharing your convictions. In newer relationships or less committed ones, it may be wiser to wait.

In all of them, though, the context of love should prevail. "A soft answer turns away wrath, but a harsh word stirs up anger" (Proverbs 15:1). As tough as it is to answer, it's always good to ask, "What do "grace and truth" look like here?"

WHAT DOES THIS MEAN FOR THE WORKPLACE?

As I mentioned already, there are some baseline practices that we all need to follow. Since gay marriage is legal in the United States and since sexuality is a protected class in the Civil Rights Act, we have specific legal obligations to follow. But that literally is the least we can do. You're more likely to ask questions like these:

- Should I post something about Pride Month? If so, what?
- Should I attend the wedding of a gay employee?
- What do I do about transgender pronouns—personally and organizationally?
- Should I list "my pronouns" in my email signature or social media profile?
- How do I respond when an employee chooses to switch genders?
- How do I lead people who view these issues so differently?

At some point, you will have to answer questions like these, even translating some of the answers into official company policies.

Here are a few thoughts to help you along the way. Mostly I'm offering up other questions to help you come to your answers.

Should I post something about Pride Month? If so, what?

Try thinking about it this way: What is the goal of a Pride Month post? If your goal is to support a specific belief, you may answer the question one way. If your goal is to communicate value, you may answer another.

Most likely, what you *want* to do with a Pride Month post is to say that LGBTQ+ people are valuable and welcome. So ask yourself, is a once-a-year post the most effective way to do that? Are there other ways to accomplish the same goal? How do you communicate value to other groups of people? Are there hints that might apply here?

Should I attend the wedding of a gay employee?

Ask yourself: "If I attend, am I condoning something I don't agree with? What does it mean, for me, to attend a wedding, anyway? If I choose not to go, what other ways could I honor and help this employee? What might it look like to value this relationship, even if I choose not to attend the wedding?"

What do I do about transgender pronouns? How do I coach my employees when it comes to trans pronouns? Should I list "my pronouns" in my email signature or social media profile?

I'll tackle these few questions together, since they all deal with the (much newer) issues of transgender identity and pronoun use.[55] As a general rule, I tend to default to using the terminology that others use for themselves. When it comes to trans identity, that means adopting the pronouns the person offers me, whether that matches their biological sex or not. Others disagree here, considering that a form of affirming and validating the trans person's choices. Still others attempt to sidestep the issue, using the person's name and trying to avoid pronouns for trans people as much as possible. None of these options are simple, and all have definite risks.

At the very least, we leaders need to be aware of the potential dynamics here. We should train our people to be aware of the pronoun conversation. And we should provide a space for those who are confused to ask questions.

How do I respond when an employee chooses to switch genders?

This gets a bit more into the nitty-gritty of policy. Suppose, for instance, a male employee of yours is transitioning to be a woman. Should this person use the women's restroom? If not, what accommodations will you make for them? At what point do you coach the rest of your team to use this person's new name and/or gender identification?

As with any area of confusion, the more clarity you can bring to a situation as a leader, the better. Think through potential answers for these questions and potential solutions for the problems they might raise. Think through it now, before it becomes a real life scenario. Then, when the situation arises, be willing to apply wisdom and adjust.

How do I lead people who view these issues so differently?

It would be tough enough if all you had to do was answer these questions for yourself. But you don't. As a leader, you have to navigate a just and loving course while you lead people who want to pull in very different directions.

My main advice here is simply to apply what you've read so far: Before you jump into what you should do, pause to consider what you need to see. Step into the shoes of your people. Learn why they hold the beliefs they do. Get to know their stories. Become adept at articulating their position, even if you disagree. If you can put on the various lenses of the people working with you, you'll be well poised to help them look at one another with charity and grace.

With confidence, we can follow God's pathway toward leaders thriving, companies thriving, and our communities thriving. While he didn't prescribe specific solutions to some of the pressing issues we're facing today, he has shown us what it looks like when justice transforms a person, a group, a city.

Before we move to our next section, I want to take a look at that transformation process in detail. It comes from the longest recorded conversation we have from the life of Jesus. And, perhaps unsurprisingly, it shows us how Jesus, the ultimate just leader, brought justice and joy to someone who least expected it.

QUESTIONS TO CONSIDER

1. What might it look like to love someone and accept them while also disagreeing with them around issues of sexuality and gender?
2. For business leaders, how do you create a culture of belonging for those in the LGBTQ+ community?
3. Who do you need to learn from to become more culturally competent in your leadership in this area?
4. How does Jesus's posture of grace *and* truth challenge you? Which area do you need to grow in? What could that look like practically?

CHAPTER 12

The Culturally Competent Leader

In the last few chapters, we've spent a lot of time talking about cultural competency: what it is, why it matters, how to build it. I know that digging into culture can be more than a little disorienting. So I want to close this section by going back to the basics. Remember, the thesis of this book is that we can grow to be just leaders because we follow Jesus, the ultimate just leader. And, ironically to many of us, the more we pursue justice, the more we thrive personally. Rather than a vicious cycle, we can find ourselves in a virtuous cycle, multiplying justice and joy wherever we go—until, in the end, the entire city can rejoice.

So how did Jesus do this? I'm glad you asked.

Jesus provides us with a model of what it looks like to be a culturally competent leader as he engages the Samaritan woman at Jacob's well in John 4.

"HE TOLD ME ALL THAT I EVER DID"

Here's the context of John 4: Jesus has just begun his public ministry. People were hearing about him and the miracles he was performing. He was with his disciples and decided to travel from Judea (in the south) to Galilee (in the north).

In between Judea and Galilee is a region called Samaria. This is where we pick up the story:

[Jesus] left Judea and departed again for Galilee. And he had to pass through Samaria. So he came to a town of Samaria called Sychar, near the field that Jacob had given to his son Joseph. Jacob's well was there; so Jesus, wearied as he was from his journey, was sitting beside the well. It was about the sixth hour. A woman from Samaria came to draw water. Jesus said to her, "Give me a drink." (John 4:3–7)

Jesus's disciples had actually left Jesus there to go into the city to buy food. The sixth hour means it was twelve noon, and it was hot. It wasn't the usual time to head to the well for water. But as we'll soon see, the woman Jesus meets isn't like most other women in town.

The Samaritan woman probably wasn't used to encountering anyone on her midday trips to the well, so she was surprised that Jesus chose to engage her at all:

"How is it that you, a Jew, ask for a drink from me, a woman of Samaria?" (For Jews have no dealings with Samaritans.)

Jesus answered her, "If you knew the gift of God, and who it is that is saying to you, 'Give me a drink,' you would have asked him, and he would have given you living water." (John 4:9–10)

They're at a well, and they're talking about water. Simple enough. But Jesus turns the conversation pretty quickly away from literal water and toward metaphorical water—living water, *spiritual* water. He offers her a saving water that would satisfy her every need. She would never be thirsty again. Jesus says to her:

"Everyone who drinks of this water will be thirsty again, but whoever drinks of the water that I will give him will never be thirsty again. The water that I will give him will become in him a spring of water welling up to eternal life."

The woman said to him, "Sir, give me this water, so that I will not be thirsty or have to come here to draw water." (John 4:13–15)

Eternal life is always an intriguing prospect, so it's not surprising that the woman expresses interest. Jesus, though, turns the conversation again. He asks her to go get her husband. Now, this is awkward for the woman because while she is technically unmarried, she is apparently living with another man. *How does this guy know all that?* This question exposes her:

The woman answered him, "I have no husband."
Jesus said to her, "You are right in saying, 'I have no husband'; for you have had five husbands, and the one you now have is not your husband. What you have said is true."
The woman said to him, "Sir, I perceive that you are a prophet." (John 4:17–19)

Despite the discomfort, the woman starts to realize there is something special about Jesus. So she dives into a theological debate, asking him about the Jews' belief that worship must take place in Jerusalem. But Jesus isn't thrown off by her question. Instead, he offers her a revolutionary thought:

"Woman, believe me, the hour is coming when neither on this mountain nor in Jerusalem will you worship the Father. You worship what you do not know; we worship what we know, for salvation is from the Jews. But the hour is coming, and is now here, when the true worshipers will worship the Father in spirit and truth, for the Father is seeking such people to worship him. God is spirit, and those who worship him must worship in spirit and truth." (John 4:21–24)

She wants to know which mountain is the right one for worship. Jesus rejects her either-or question, letting her know that true worship of God is not bound to a place, or even to a certain people group. Instead, it is available to anyone who believes in him and worships him in spirit and truth.

The woman is beginning to realize that this man may be more than just a prophet. And soon she has her suspicions confirmed:

> "I know that Messiah is coming (he who is called Christ). When he comes, he will tell us all things."
> Jesus said to her, "I who speak to you am he." (John 4:25–26)

Right at the pinnacle of their conversation, the disciples wander back from their trip into the city. Unsurprisingly, they marvel that Jesus was talking to a woman (and a Samaritan woman at that!). They do not ask him why he had been speaking with her; they just keep their thoughts to themselves.

The woman, on the other hand, has bolted into the city, not even realizing she left her water jar—the very purpose for which she had gone to the well! She immediately began telling everyone to come see the man who "told me all that I ever did." She wondered, "Could he be the Christ?"

So that lonely little well suddenly became very crowded: Jesus, his disciples, the Samaritan woman, and crowds of people from town all bunched together. Many people believed in Jesus that day. All because of the woman's simple testimony, "He told me all that I ever did."

We're not likely to be traveling on foot from Jerusalem to Galilee, but there are still some solid gold principles in this story. At the Samaritan well, Jesus gave us ten principles for what it looks like to be a culturally competent leader.

1. He Was Intentional. The story said that Jesus *had* to go through Samaria. *Had* is an interesting choice of word. He didn't really have to go through Samaria. Even though Samaria was on the way, he was not in a hurry. Plus, everyone at that time knew that Jews *always* went around Samaria when they traveled from Judea to Galilee.

Why did they do this? As John mentioned in this story, Jews hated Samaritans. They considered Samaritans half-breeds, half-dead, religious sell-outs, unclean. Associating with Samaritans in any way would be unconscionable and make them unclean. So, they never went through Samaria. They *had* to go around.

But not Jesus. Jesus *had to go through* Samaria. Jesus had another purpose. He took an intentional, uncomfortable, and even dangerous step to journey through Samaria. But he did so with the mindset to break down the walls between Jews and Samaritans.

Where is our "Samaria"? Who are our "Samaritans"? They are places in our communities that are foreign to us. They are people we dislike or who make us uncomfortable. What intentional steps do we need to take to go to them and break down those walls?

2. He Acknowledged Her Value. Through his intentionality and the way he engaged her, Jesus treated the woman like an image bearer of God. He understood her unique value and did not treat her as "the other." She was astounded that he even spoke to her. His apostles were astounded that he spoke to her. Jews didn't talk with Samaritans. Men didn't talk with women they had never met. For Jesus's earliest followers, none would have chosen her as the first person to learn about Jesus's messianic identity. And yet, Jesus doesn't care a whit about all that. He saw her, he had a conversation with her, and he demonstrated care. He did not overlook her or feel that she was unworthy of his time and attention. It's possible he was the first person to do this in years.

Culturally competent leaders understand everyone's value and dignity. They engage people purposefully to uplift that value. They are careful not to be guided by internal biases they have for others and instead treat people as they are—image bearers of God.

3. He Knew the Culture and the Context. Jesus was very familiar with the dynamic between Jews and Gentiles. He also understood how unique it was for a man to interact with a woman in that setting. He would have been keenly aware of the dicey situation he was walking into. And that's precisely why he did it. He knew what he was doing, and he had to know the context to engage it appropriately.

As leaders, we have to be students of history and know the cultural context of our communities and cities in which we live. Learning about that cultural context might initially make us nervous: *What if we make a mistake? Are we honoring this culture appropriately?* But if we press into that discomfort, we can come out the other side with renewed confidence in our cross-cultural abilities. We can, like Jesus, read the culture and step into the culture.

4. He Gave Power Away. Jesus asked her for a drink. This is one of the most profound statements in the story, though modern readers are likely to skip right past it. Some people read that part and feel it has a tone of being demanding, like he is ordering a subordinate to serve him. But the way he interacts with her suggests a much different tone.

Remember, it would be unheard of for a Jew to ask a Samaritan for help, much less a man asking a woman to help him. And it's not as though she turns on the faucet, fills a cup, and hands it to him. Getting water out of a deep well is hard work. Jesus was tired, and he asked her to help him. He asked her to be strong for him. And in doing so, he gave her power.

This is one of the most significant steps a leader can take to be culturally competent—particularly a leader who is a part of the majority culture. There are all kinds of ways to think about power and how we can give it away. In fact, we'll cover this much more when we get to Quality 3.

5. He Listened to Her. As God, Jesus already knew everything about this woman and her story. He didn't need to ask questions and wait patiently for her answers. And yet, his conversation with her was personal and engaging. He asked questions and listened, truly listened. He did not generalize or lump her into a category. He found out her needs, the way she thought, and what was important to her. He treated her as an individual.

Culturally competent leaders listen and treat people as individuals. They take the time to get to know them, ask good questions, and refrain from putting them in a category. After all, if the omniscient God of the universe thought it was worth his time to get to know a single person, how much more should we?

6. He Built Trust with Her. Over the course of their conversation, the way Jesus engaged with the woman built trust. He didn't lead with, "You know, everything you believe about God is wrong." No, he was gentle and understood her perspective. He gained the opportunity to speak into her life.

Trust is huge if we ever intend to cross cultures. It takes time, patience, and a willingness to enter into people's lives. I learned this with Shay, as I mentioned in Chapter 6. I had no idea she had reason not to trust me at the beginning of our relationship. For me, if I was going to build trust with her, I could not approach her as a project. I needed to see her as a person and take the steps necessary to trust her.

7. He Spoke Truth to Her. Jesus called out the woman's sin. He exposed that she was currently living with someone who was not her husband and before that, she had had five husbands. Granted, we don't know the circumstances behind those five marriages. Maybe the husbands died. Maybe the husbands mistreated her. Maybe they were the ones who left (after all, serving divorce papers wasn't something women could do in the first century). We aren't told all of her backstory. But we do know the woman was clearly not eager to share about her marital history. Jesus, however, went there anyway.

Culturally competent leaders don't overlook truth to bridge gaps. Gaps can't be bridged if we avoid the truth. We live in a world where truth is often thought of as relative. Your truth is your truth and my truth is my truth. While that feels loving, it's not. Not if we know what is true and know that truth is defined not by us, but by God. Real relationship is built on truth, even uncomfortable truth. It can never be built on lies, no matter how comforting they are.

Jesus not only called out her sin, but he also shared with her that he was the living water and if she believed in him, she would never be thirsty again. In other words, he spoke truth, but also offered grace.

It's incumbent on us, then, to speak truth gently, without condemnation, to help people see who God really is and how he operates in the world.

8. He Communicated Clearly, Precisely, and Graciously. Jesus did not use sweeping statements like we see in our culture today. *All Samaritans are like this. You Samaritan women constantly say stuff like that.* No, Jesus was very precise, even surgical, cutting through the complexity and nuance of what he needed to say to the woman. Because he did not lump her into a category, he spoke to her particular situation and addressed her particular thoughts and ideas.

Crossing cultures requires clear, precise, and gracious communication. We can't be lazy in how we talk; we can't overstate issues that are nuanced and complicated. We need to mean what we say and say what we mean.

9. He Was Misunderstood by His Disciples. When the disciples returned, they didn't know why he was talking to the woman. The text even says they *questioned* what he was doing (though they didn't tell him that). Sounds like some of our friends, right? On the outside they seem OK with us pressing into issues of justice, but on the inside, they are criticizing us.

People who cross cultures are often misunderstood, even by their closest friends. That's because it's common for people who are crossing cultural divides to take actions that are against the norm or unusual. (Do you recall anyone else chatting it up with this woman at the well? Nope—just Jesus.)

Those who *aren't* stepping across cultural lines can't quite see why you are doing what you are doing. Their default, then, is to criticize or judge.

It is common to be lonely if you are a leader who's committed to building bridges across cultures. It's also common to feel tired and worn out. I mean, what happens to bridges? *They get walked on.* And that hurts.

For me, I can find it difficult to belong. I don't identify with one group, because if I did, it would mean I don't identify with *another* group that I also care about. So I find myself in between many groups that are different from one another. And being a part of many groups (particularly at the fringe) can make me feel like I'm a part of *none* of them. That's tough.

I can feel isolated, misunderstood, lonely, and overlooked. The natural response is to wonder, *What's wrong with me? Why did I not get invited? Did I say something wrong? How come it looks much easier over there than over here?*

But just leaders recognize the call, culturally and spiritually, to be the bridge between different groups. To be the bridge between culturally different employees, between our organization and the community, between those with plenty and those in poverty. Chasms are growing all around us. If leaders will not stand in the gap, who will?

10. He Started Small. Jesus's goal in his interaction with the Samaritan woman was to spread the gospel beyond Jerusalem and Judea, to Samaria and to the ends of the world. If you were to ask one of the disciples how Jesus was going to accomplish that lofty goal, you'd probably find a different strategy than having a random conversation with a random Samaritan woman at a random well in the middle of the day.

But through this one woman, many Samaritans believed. Jesus's small step led to something bigger than we'd expect. Not only did many follow Jesus that day, but this story has been passed down for centuries, helping fuel a worldwide spread of the gospel that has been made available to you and me today.

We can feel paralyzed by the widespread division in our world. How can we bridge these cultures? How can we overcome injustice? It's all simply too big! And because that overwhelms us, we often choose to do nothing.

But Jesus shows us that we don't have to pursue a master plan designed to impact the masses. We can—in fact, we must—start small, even with just one person.

QUESTIONS TO CONSIDER

1. Which of the qualities Jesus demonstrates do you identify with the most?
2. Which quality challenges you the most?
3. Where is your "Samaria"—the place out of your comfort zone that you have to go to? Where are you "the other" or "the only one"?
4. What steps can you take to build relationships across lines of cultural difference? Who might be one person for you to engage?

QUALITY 3

GIVE POWER AWAY

In his book, *Playing God: Redeeming the Gift of Power*, Andy Crouch compares power to electricity: Those who have the most of it rarely think about it—until suddenly it goes away.[56]

You probably live in a home surrounded by electricity. It's central to nearly everything you do: It keeps your food cold and your house warm; it allows you to watch television and browse around on the internet; it helps you wash your clothes and wake up before dawn. But chances are, you don't actively think about electricity very often.

The exception? During a power outage. When a blizzard or thunderstorm knocks out the electricity on your block, suddenly you become keenly aware of everything electricity has to offer.

When it comes to power, most of us think of it about as often as we think about our electricity. We aren't attuned to it. It's not something we recognize on a daily basis. We may even begin to think it's not terribly important to us—just as someone sitting in a perfectly heated home might naively assume that just because he doesn't much *think* about electricity, he doesn't much *benefit* from it, either.

Unlike electricity, we *all* have some measure of power. But for many of us, we only begin to think about our power when we have a metaphorical "power outage."

On the other hand, many voices in our culture seem patently obsessed with power. Perhaps they are angling for more and more of it, trying to position themselves as the strongest or the most capable. Perhaps they are gathering as much money as they can as a way of growing in power. Perhaps they are striving to gain more and more authority. In this kind of dog-eat-dog view of power, all that matters is getting what you want and controlling others.

No wonder, then, that so many people tend to think of power as inherently evil.

Just leaders are not led down any of these false roads. They are not ignorant of power, pretending it doesn't exist. They are not greedy for power, gobbling up more and more of it. But neither are they opposed to power, assuming it is evil. All of those views of power are incredibly limited.

In contrast, just leaders see power the way God does. God's view and demonstration of power is much more comprehensive and contrary than the ways we normally think of power. And, it turns out, much more life-giving, too—not just for others, but for all of us.

Once we understand God's power, we can become the type of just leaders who begin to give it away.

CHAPTER 13

Where's the Power?

When it comes to board games, I'm not a huge fan of Monopoly. I was more of a Risk guy growing up, but when I had the opportunity to play Monopoly, I always lost (I wasn't patient enough to get through a whole game). But even though I lost, I still enjoyed the feeling of owning property. Here I was, seven years old, and maybe I didn't have Park Place or Boardwalk, but I owned an *entire railroad*. What seven-year-old could say that?

One of the basics of the game of Monopoly—one I understood before anyone even explained the game to me—is that the game is about *getting*. Get more money, more property, more utilities, all of it. At no point in the game was I tempted to simply *give away* the stuff I had. You simply can't win that way.

I'm no longer a seven-year-old playing Monopoly with my brother and sister, but somehow, very little has changed in my heart. Giving things away—whether it's time, money, skill, or power—is still an uphill climb.

I suspect I'm not the only one.

Just leaders do a lot of things with their power. But one of the most significant is that they give that power away. That sounds nice in principle, but it's not the way our culture operates. Our culture these days is all about power. Who has it? Who doesn't? How can I get *more* of it? In a power-saturated culture like ours, suggesting that someone give their power away sounds foolish (at best) or harmful (at worst).

I believe there are two counterfeit views of power that make it tough for us to see God's power for what it is. Like all counterfeits, they initially seem compelling. But they're false; so in the end, they never deliver what they promise. The just approach to power (which is also the most flourishing approach) charts a different course.

Let's take a look at the counterfeits.

COUNTERFEIT #1: POWER AS IDENTITY

I did a quick Google search for the word *power* in advertisements. Literally, this took me less than five minutes, and these were some of the most common messages:

- Don't let anyone take your power away from you.
- The only time you don't have power is when you give it away.
- Do not give your power away to others, asking them to define you.
- Claim your power!

The messaging here is pretty clear: Your power matters, so don't you dare give it away.

The main problem here is that these messages equate a person's *power* with their *identity* and *value*. And if that's the case, you can see why it would be wrong to let others take it from you. None of us wants to be controlled or defined by others, especially others with agendas we dislike.

But power and identity aren't interchangeable.

There's another view of power—a healthier and more nuanced view— that is more a matter of *authority*. In this view, power is not a synonym for "who you are" but a recognition of ability or capacity. Think of money, for example, as a tangible form of power: Someone with one hundred dollars has more purchasing ability—purchasing power—than someone with twenty dollars. Or think of physical strength: I can bench press 150 pounds; a friend who hits the gym more than me can most likely bench 250 pounds. He's got more ability—lifting *power*—than me.

If power is about identity, then we're all going to be naturally protective of it. But if power is more about *ability*, then we can be free to think of it differently. After all, our identity is already settled, and it has nothing to do with our abilities. Our identity is marked by the eternal value of being created in God's image and adopted into God's family.

COUNTERFEIT #2: POWER AS DOMINATION

Power, in essence, is about *authority* and *ability*. So far so good. But authority introduces another warped view of power: authoritarianism. This is what many of us think of when we hear the word power—not as a neutral category dealing with someone's potential, but as a toxic category describing domination. When we think of power, many of us don't think of the power to (say, the power to lift 250 pounds) but of power over (say, the power to harm or intimidate others). From this vantage point, power is domination, oppression, coercion.

If power is mainly about domination, then giving it away doesn't really fix the problem. Redistributing oppressive power only creates new oppressors. History has given us more than enough examples to show us how unhelpful that carousel is. Oppressive power doesn't get better because someone else has it. We need a different approach.

So, we shouldn't be giving away power-as-identity or power-as-domination. What, then, are we supposed to give away? What exactly is God's power?

GOD'S POWER: CREATIVE, VULNERABLE, UPLIFTING

God's power, as we see it in Scripture, is creative, vulnerable, and uplifting.

1. God's Power Is Creative. The Bible begins with God exercising his power. But he's not impressing us with how much he can bench-press or how many dollars are in his bank account. He's flinging planets into outer space and speaking stars into existence. With the possible exception of Jesus's resurrection, there is no display of power that comes close to the power of Genesis 1.

God says a word. That's it. And from the void, literally everything appears. That is power.

While we may be more familiar with power that controls and compels, we should never skip the fact that God's first exercise of power was to create. When we exercise power in our world, we can do the same. No, we can't speak planets into existence. But we can take the raw materials of God's creation and cultivate something new—new laws, new products, new connections, new projects. Any time we use the skills God has given us to bring something new into the world, we follow in the footsteps of God's creative power.

2. God's Power Is Vulnerable. Andy Crouch, in *Playing God*, points out that true human flourishing comes when we combine authority *and* vulnerability. We tend to think of these two ideas as competitors: Either we have power and authority or we are weak and vulnerable. But Crouch argues that we become fully human—that we thrive most fully—when we experience both together.

Why does this matter to power? Because Jesus combined both authority and vulnerability in his life. Jesus shows us that power doesn't have to be dominating; it can be disarming. This is how the Apostle Paul put it:

Jesus did not count equality with God a thing to be grasped, but emptied himself, by taking the form of a servant . . . and he humbled himself by becoming obedient to the point of death, even death on a cross. (Philippians 2:6–8)

In becoming human, Jesus became patently *vulnerable*. He experienced all the same pains and struggles we do. He got tired. He got sick. In the end, he died—and it was a much more horrific and lonely death than any of us can even imagine.

And yet, even as Jesus endured all of this, he never once lost his authority as God's Son. He spoke with authority. He healed with authority. He remained full of creative power, even as he took on a vulnerable form for us.

Ironically, by becoming vulnerable, Jesus did something he never could have done if he remained safely in heaven: He saved us. This is one of the surprises of God's vulnerable power: By exposing himself to risk, even death, God accomplished something more magnificent, more powerful, than he ever could have by playing it safe.

3. God's Power Is Uplifting. Jesus didn't just make himself vulnerable. He did it for a reason. He went low, he served, he decreased *so that others would increase.* He disadvantaged himself for the advantage of others: "For you know the grace of our Lord Jesus Christ, that though he was rich, **yet for your sake he became poor**, so that you by his poverty might become rich" (2 Corinthians 8:9, emphasis added).

As just leaders, we are called to do the same. We know that all of our power and influence comes from God. We follow God by emptying ourselves so we can lift others up. This is a power that allows us to die to ourselves, disadvantaging ourselves because we know that success is not found in the way the world measures success. It's no longer about how we compare to others, who's the best, who has the most, or who has achieved the most.

No, success comes by emptying ourselves for the sake of others so that all people flourish—particularly those who are broken, hurting, and overlooked.

Jesus said, "Whoever loses their life for my sake will find it" (Matthew 10:39, NIV).

And Paul wrote to the Philippians, "For me to live is Christ, and to die is gain" (Philippians 1:21).

This is where we can start to give our power away.

When all of us get to the point where we want to lose and die to ourselves, then everyone wins, *including* us. There is no zero-sum game with winners and losers. That's dominating power. That's the world's power. But with God's power, the pie gets bigger. Giving power multiplies power for everyone.

NOT LESS POWERFUL, BUT DIFFERENTLY POWERFUL

Admittedly, the idea of giving power away can be really challenging for those who have been deeply oppressed. The pain and trauma of oppression cannot be overlooked. Nor should we ignore the need for justice and accountability.

Only if we see power God's way—as creative, vulnerable, uplifting— can we give it away without ultimately losing it.

Consider Dr. Martin Luther King Jr. The Civil Rights Movement was powerful because Dr. King demanded justice from oppression, and yet he led a nonviolent movement that respected all people, even those oppressing him.

Or think of Nelson Mandela, who learned Afrikaans, the language of his oppressors, to gain their mutual respect. This ultimately positioned him to lead South Africa out of apartheid.

Or consider Jesus himself, who took on the ultimate oppression— condemnation and death—so we could have life.

What all three of these examples have in common (among other things) is that even as they gave their power away, they remained people of authority. To put it differently, the way they viewed power, it clearly wasn't a zero-sum game.

When most people hear "give away power," they imagine that we're asking them to do without, to simply have less. And in the short term, that may often be the case. But the bigger picture is that true power-sharing does not make us less powerful; it makes us *differently* powerful. It makes our power less like Satan's (destructive and coercive) and more like God's (creative, life-giving, and uplifting).

How do we follow Jesus's example and become poor so others might be rich? Personally, I think of forgiving people who are hard to forgive and have harmed me, laying down my preferences for the preferences of others, sacrificing something I love, and letting go of my money in a way that hurts.

But I'm getting a bit ahead of myself. First, let's take a look at how this renewed vision of power should change our leadership.

QUESTIONS TO CONSIDER
1. Which counterfeit of power do you believe the most?
2. How have you seen power be creative? vulnerable? uplifting?
3. What are ways you can begin to use power differently in your leadership?

CHAPTER 14

Power and Leadership

According to Gallup, a staggering 67 percent of employees are not engaged at their job.[57] Sixty-nine percent leave not because of their jobs but because of their . . . bosses.[58]

Something their bosses did or failed to do. Ouch.

If we were to ask those 69 percent of bosses, I doubt we'd find any that want to create a terrible work environment. But there's a huge gap between our desires and our realities.

If you have any influence at all, you need to accept that your work culture is an overflow of your own decisions and habits. Who *you* are becomes who *your organization* is. So if you're constantly running on fumes, guess what? You're probably part of the 69 percent.

The good news is you don't have to stay there. You can grow into a just leader who *thrives* in the workplace, rather than just *surviving* in it. Because if you're thriving, it'll become much easier to create an environment in which your employees thrive.

So, let's have a real moment: How are you doing? Would you say you're thriving? If so, why? If not, why not?

Think of it another way: Do you *love* what you are doing right now? Are you excited when you wake up on Monday morning knowing you have a full week of work ahead—or do you dread it?

Actually, let's take it a step further: Take a moment to review the words below and identify the ones that describe the way you feel on a Monday morning. Check all that apply. This is your book. Go for it.

When I begin my workweek, I feel . . .

- Excited
- Grateful
- Unhurried
- Focused
- Filled with ideas
- Content
- In a hurry
- Bored
- Distracted
- Overwhelmed
- Anxious
- Frustrated
- Tired

Maybe you're still struggling to pinpoint how you feel about your current work. Here are a few more diagnostic questions. See if you can find yourself somewhere in here:

- Are you invigorated by the work you get to do and the people with whom you get to work? Or are you bored, frustrated, even exhausted?
- Do you think about work all the time? Can you separate work from the rest of life, so you can get away and have a vacation—a true vacation where you are unplugged from the office and not looking at emails, texts, or your phone?
- How are you sleeping? Do you sleep well or do you find yourself tossing and turning because of the anxiety you feel at work?
- Do you trust your people to get the job done, giving you the time and space to think strategically, work on your business, and plan for the future?
- Are you able to give priority to your family and pay attention to their needs?

- How would your spouse and/or children answer these questions about you? Would they say you are thriving?

The point here isn't to heap shame on you. I've had some rough answers to all of these questions in my career. The goal here is just to audit where you *actually* are. This is a starting point.

So let's get started.

To help us and those we lead to thrive, I want to unpack six THRIVE qualities by walking through the word THRIVE: Trust, Health, Relationships, Impact, Value, Engagement. As we go through these, I want you to identify the areas where you are doing well and where you need to grow.

TRUST

Thriving begins with trust. Do you have a deep sense of trust in the people you are leading and do they trust you? What do you do to foster trust and how do your people know you trust them?

According to the Center for Creative Leadership, when trust is present, people step forward and do their best work together and efficiently. They align around a common purpose, take risks, think out of the box, have one another's backs, and communicate openly and honestly.[59]

But when trust is absent, people jockey for position, hoard information, play it safe, and talk *about*—rather than *to*—one another. Not only is this a miserable way to work, but it also undermines everything that makes work, well, *work*. An environment of suspicion kills creativity, productivity, and problem solving.

Trust (or the lack of it) can be a hard thing to measure. But we can watch for signals. Here's what a lack of trust tends to look like: Leaders with low trust end up doing work they should not be doing. Conversely, they refrain from empowering their people and giving them more responsibility. In the short term, you may be able to achieve a lot this way. But in the long term, it'll only lead to burnout (for you) and disengagement (for your team). And burned out, disengaged teammates aren't primed to build trust. It's a vicious cycle.

The irony here is that most employees truly *want* more responsibility and more opportunities to grow. Very few employees want to do the bare minimum (though some, of course, do). Leaders tend to underestimate their employees' hunger for greater challenges. So leaders end up getting in the way—because they do not fully trust their people.

You don't have to hand over the keys to your entire empire to everyone. And certainly you need to be intentional to train your people well so they can effectively accomplish the responsibilities you give them. But start with something small today. Share responsibility. Share initiative. Take the first step of trusting your team—and watch to see how they respond. You may be surprised at what happens next.

HEALTH

Are you healthy? Physically, emotionally, and spiritually? Are you getting enough sleep? Are you exercising regularly? Are you "too busy" to get away and take a break?

Do you hear questions like this and think to yourself, *I'm not even sure any of that is possible?*

In her article "The Way We Work Is Killing Us," Brigid Schulte reports that in the United States, employees work among the longest, most extreme, and most irregular hours; they have no guarantee for paid sick days, paid vacation, or paid family leave; and they pay more for health insurance yet are sicker and more stressed out than workers in other advanced economies.[60]

She interviewed Jeffrey Pfeffer, the author of *Dying for a Paycheck* and a professor of organizational behavior at the Stanford Graduate School of Business. He says:

Companies are completely missing the point. Offering lunchtime yoga to stressed-out workers ignores the real reason why workers are so stressed out in the first place—management practices like long work hours, unpredictable schedules, toxic bosses, and after-hours emails. It's not individual workers making bad choices about their health that's making them so sick. It's the way corporate America expects workers to work.

The thing about workplace culture is that it's caught more than it's taught. If our employees are stressed out and overworked, it's probably not because we made them go through a seminar about "How to Work Yourself into the Ground." More likely, they picked up that pace of overwork *from us.*

So let me ask you: Are you working out of your rest or are you just resting from your work?

We brought this up in Chapter 4 when we talked about Zacchaeus. Let's review: People who *work out of their rest* recognize that God is in control of every aspect of their lives, especially their work. Therefore, they are at rest: They are content, free, and calm, even when times are rough. They trust God's promises and are confident in the security he offers. The biblical idea of Sabbath—of resting from our work—is the *first* day of the week, the fuel that propels them into work, rather than the last day of the week, a crash landing after a frantic week of hustle. We work, therefore, out of the reality that we are OK, our future is secure, and nothing we do with our work adds anything to our truest identity.

When we *work out of our rest*, rest comes first. When rest comes first, we are less anxious. When rest comes first, we have a moderate pace to our work. When rest comes first, we find that we are less likely to say we're "too busy." When rest comes first, we are able to pay attention to details, able to rest and sleep well, freed up to spend time with hobbies, engage with and pay attention to our spouse and children, spend time with our friends, and take awesome vacations.

Can you remember the last time you felt like this? Can you even imagine it?

You can probably paint the picture of the opposite as well as I can. When rest is last, exhaustion, stress, and anxiety are our constant companions. When rest is last, we can't keep up with everything. When rest is last, we hold on to work too tightly, unable to take breaks or use our PTO. When rest is last, we think about work *all the time*; we just can't get it out of our heads, even when we're "off the clock." When rest is last, we give our spouse and children our leftovers, we're distracted on vacations, we spend little (or no) time on hobbies, and we may have poor health.

I find many of the leaders I work with feel they have to demonstrate long hours and be available all of the time because they believe that's the way they will get their people to work hard. They feel they have to be the model. These leaders are right—and they're wrong. They are absolutely right that they have to be the model. But they are wrong in what they think they need to model. Our employees don't need to strive after the pattern of overwhelmed, strung out, and unhealthy work. What people need to see instead are healthy leaders who have a proper perspective of work.

RELATIONSHIPS

Do you have healthy relationships, both at work and (more importantly) outside of work? Do people know you? Are you willing to let them in?

If you're married, how is your relationship with your spouse? If you have kids, how is your relationship with them? Do you have solid peer friendships? And how close are you to the people you are leading?

Let's unpack three of your vital relationships.

1. Your spouse and children: We can't be people of justice at work or in the community if we are not people of justice at home. We can do all this great work "out there," but if our home is not in order and our marriage and relationships with our children are not what they should be, it's really difficult, if not impossible, to be just.

How healthy is your marriage? Do you two really know each other and love to be together? Is it easy to spend time together or are you like two ships passing in the night? Are you vulnerable and intimate with one another?

And if you have children, are you present with them? Not just physically but mentally and emotionally? Are you distracted when you're with them and feel like they are interrupting you, or are you all there, completely with them and for them?

2. Your peers: We mentioned this in Chapter 5 when we talked about why leaders fail. Two of the main reasons: 1) They choose isolation over community and 2) They stop confessing their sins. Do you have close peer relationships? People who truly know you? Individuals with whom you regularly confess sin and who would do anything for you?

When my father died, I was reminded of the friendships I have developed over time; people from all parts of my life expressed their sympathy. But two friends reminded me that they would do anything for me. My close friend from college Erik, when he heard the news, got on a plane and spent the whole day with me and my family, making sure we were OK. Mostly he was simply present for whatever we needed. He didn't offer to come or ask to come. He just came.

Then there was Paul and his wife, Gwen. Paul has been a dear friend, brother, and mentor of mine throughout my career. He showed me what it truly means to trust God. Just prior to the COVID-19 pandemic, Paul had kidney failure and received a kidney transplant through a precarious (and what turned out to be dangerous) procedure, receiving his son's kidney. As a result, Paul was immunocompromised and did not leave his back porch much at all during the pandemic.

On the morning of my father's funeral, I texted Paul the link to the livestream of the service so he could watch it. This was the text I received back: "I'm en route to stand with you in your time of grief. I love you much and am praying for grace, mercy, and strength."

Paul and Gwen were already on the road, from two hours away—one of the first times Paul had left his back porch in almost two years. Just thirty minutes after receiving that text, they walked into the church.

I lost it.

Proverbs 18:24 says, "A man of many companions may come to ruin, but there is a friend who sticks closer than a brother."

Do you have those types of friendships?

3. Those you lead: We have already looked at the Johari Window and talked about the ways leaders need to be more open and vulnerable with those they lead. And in the last chapter, we saw how vulnerability is, in God's economy, a way of exercising power.

The more significant your role in your organization, the more inertia will pull you away from vulnerability. In my work with CEOs, many of them feel like they need to have it all together. They think they need to give the impression that they are good, they're strong, and all is well. I get it: They want to exude confidence so the people they lead know they're in good hands. As a result, these leaders keep a distance from their people.

The trouble is that people need much more than a show of confidence. They need connection, trust, authenticity. And the more a leader maintains a veneer of perfection, the less people are willing to follow. Leaders need to be real, authentic, show weakness, admit mistakes, and be approachable.

Does this mean you need to become best friends with all of your co-workers or employees? Of course not. But don't overlook the need for relational connection. It's not a waste of your time. It's not something you have to *get through* to get to your real work. In a very real sense, these relationships *are* your work; they are what makes your organization thrive.

Are you willing to be vulnerable with your people? What keeps you from letting people see who you really are?

IMPACT

Back in Chapter 5, we briefly mentioned the reality that work is a part of our DNA; it's the way we are made. When God created people, he gave them a job—to fill the earth and subdue it, rule over the fish of the sea, the birds of the air, and everything that roams over the ground. What that means is we are *co-creators* with God when we work.

You might think, *Co-creators? What does that even mean?* It means that God handed us the baton so we could continue his creation. All of the human innovations we see around us are the results of God using each one of us to make his creation grow. He could have created computers at the beginning of time, or cars, or furniture, or refrigerators, or pencils, or lights—but he stopped. He rested. His work of creation was done, and he handed us the keys. And now, through our work, we continue his creation.

Do you have a greater sense of how your work is impacting the world? You are carrying out God's creation, no matter how small or big the task. Because you are a co-creator, every task is of utmost importance.

Strong leaders help their people understand the impact of their work. Not only in the grand scheme of things (like continuing God's creation) but in the overall purpose and direction of the company or organization. They tie everyone's role to the mission and vision they are pursuing.

Rob realized he needed to do something to help his employees recognize the impact of their work. He runs a steel fabricating business, and he sensed the need to breathe life into his employees, particularly those employees who did back-office work and didn't see the end results of their efforts. So he and his team planned a company meeting at one of their signature projects—a newly designed, state-of-the-art train station made with their steel.

Every employee was present to get a behind-the-scenes tour of the station so they could see how every single task performed by every single employee—from processing a document, to calculating a measurement, to working with the customer, to sourcing the steel, to shaping the steel to fit—led to the development of this extraordinary building.

Just seeing it was enough to inject life and purpose into every aspect of their work.

Are you inspired and motivated by the greater impact you are having on the world through your work? Are you helping your people understand that every task they do, even the mundane ones, contributes to the overall mission and vision you are pursuing?

VALUE

Do you feel valued? Do you matter?

Yes, you. Even if you are the CEO or in a key leadership position, it's important that you realize your own worth. Do you? Do you understand and experience how valuable you are? Or do you let the way people interact with you diminish your value? Do you value what you do and instill that value into the people you lead?

Dr. Martin Luther King Jr. once said, "No work is insignificant. All labor that uplifts humanity has dignity and importance and should be undertaken with painstaking excellence." We tend to create hierarchies for work, with certain jobs mattering more than others. And while there may be good reasons to pay some positions differently than others, we should never imply that certain kinds of work are devoid of value.

But I have a warning for you. We can value our work too much.

In 2019, Derek Thompson wrote in *The Atlantic* that the "religion of workism" was making Americans patently miserable.[61] Technically, "workism" isn't a literal religion. But the way many American workers function, it might as well be. Workism is the belief that work is not only necessary to economic production, but also the centerpiece of one's identity and life's purpose.

That doesn't sound particularly harmful, does it? What's wrong with finding purpose in my work? After all, the old adage goes, "Find a job you love, and you'll never work a day in your life."

The old adage, it turns out, is a recipe for burnout.

The best-educated and highest-earning Americans, who can have *whatever they want*, give themselves over to work because it's where they feel most themselves. At first, this is thrilling and fulfilling. But it's not long before the joy they find in their work turns into an obsession. That's what always happens when we hang our identity somewhere: Whatever gives us identity rules our lives. If that identity is rooted in God, then our lives are marked by flourishing. But if that identity is rooted anywhere else—money, family, or in this case, career—it turns sour.

We Christians aren't even the loudest voices pointing this out, either. Around the same time as Thompson's article, Anne Helen Peterson wrote a scathing article on *Buzzfeed News* showing how millennials—the bulk of the current workforce—have funneled most of their dreams of self-actualization into salaried jobs . . . and what they've received in return is collective anxiety, mass disappointment, and inevitable burnout.[62]

There is nothing wrong with elevating the dignity and value of work. God created work, and it is good. But our identity can't rest there.

ENGAGEMENT

And finally, engagement. Lots has been written about employee engagement, especially since disengagement is so high. Gallup, for instance, has developed the Q12 survey[63] which gauges twelve critical aspects for companies to evaluate employee engagement. It's an extremely helpful resource.

In addition, the Job Characteristics Model,[64] developed in 1975 by organizational psychologists Greg R. Oldham and J. Richard Hackman, is a universal model that is still used today to improve employee engagement. Oldham and Hackman found that if a job has the five qualities listed below, it will be more engaging and keep the employee happier and more productive:

1. **Skills Variety**—the amount of variety in any one job
2. **Task Identity**—a clear beginning, middle, and end to a job task
3. **Task Significance**—the level of impact the job has on the company and its customers
4. **Task Autonomy**—the amount of independence an employee has to complete the job
5. **Job Feedback**—the extent to which employees understand how well they are performing

Being diligent to position employees with work that has these characteristics will increase engagement. It will also allow you to see where people do their best work and complement others' skill sets. And most importantly, it will allow you to position your people to see how they can grow and develop in their jobs. No one wants to be in a dead-end job.

If leaders can use their power to help their people be productive, do what they do best, and be motivated to grow, they shouldn't be surprised when they start to see thriving employees, thriving companies, and thriving communities.

QUESTIONS TO CONSIDER

1. Are you thriving as a leader? Why or why not?
2. In what areas are you thriving the most? How about the least? (Trust, Health, Relationships, Impact, Value, Engagement)
3. What steps do you need to take to thrive as a leader?
4. What steps do you need to take to help *your people* thrive?

CHAPTER 15

Power and Money

I'm going to go out on a limb here and guess that this chapter makes you deeply nervous. After all, I opened this section on power with the claim that just leaders *give their power away*. And in many ways, money is a tangible form of power. So whether you're excited about it (unlikely) or bracing for it (likely), either way you're already anticipating that I'm going to say, "Give a bunch of your money away," right?

Not exactly.

Sure, giving away money matters. But the intersection of justice, power, and money is a bit more complicated than that.

I probably don't need to convince you that much of the injustice we see in our world today is deeply connected to the abuse of power and the love of money. So, if we want our city to rejoice, at some point we need to address money. But before we get into the specifics of how we can use money for justice (rather than injustice), let's consider some more fundamental questions.

- How do you feel about money? Do you think about it often? Rarely? Are you cold and calculating about it—all business? Does talking about money leave you feeling guilty or ashamed? Or the opposite— proud and confident?
- How about the money you have? Do you feel like you have enough? Do you wish you had more? Would you be one of the few who could say you have more than enough of it?

- Do you hold on to your money? Do you find yourself to be stingy? Or do you hold your money loosely and feel free to be generous with it? Which posture characterizes your view of money better—a closed fist or an open hand?

THE REAL PROBLEM WITH MONEY

I had the opportunity to lead a workshop recently with a friend of mine, Will. This workshop was geared toward leaders who were learning how to connect authentically with people of wealth. Will is a person of wealth, and he and I had developed a deep friendship when I led Jobs for Life. He was one of JfL's donors.

As a nonprofit leader, it was easy for me to have a love/hate relationship with money. With the salary I made and the needs of my family, I usually operated from a scarcity mentality rather than an abundance mentality when it came to money. Despite my privilege, I never felt we had much extra to spend. Especially with four children, we only had enough to cover the basics.

As a result, I often was stressed about not having enough money for my family as well as our organization and employees. I quickly had to become extremely comfortable with raising money and developing both the skill and mindset to invite people to invest their money in our organization.

Most people hate asking people to give money, but when someone decides to give, it's so satisfying and affirming. To know that people believe in you and what you are doing enough to invest their resources is an opportunity for huge celebration. In fact, I have danced, jumped up and down, and run circles outside celebrating gifts we received from committed donors.

Donors like Will.

As Will and I began our workshop, he said something that floored all of us. I had asked him what he struggles with the most as a person of wealth.

His response? "You know, it's easy to make money. That's not the problem. Having money is actually the problem."

We all looked at one another with dumbfounded looks on our faces—basically with an expression of "What did he say? Did I hear that right? Did he say *having* money is a problem?" I felt like I could read the minds of every person in the room. We were all thinking, *If that's a problem, I'd like to see what it's like to experience that problem!*

Will went on to describe how disorienting and confusing it can be to be wealthy. People often assign value to you just because of the money you have. You feel alone. You struggle to make authentic friendships. People are always asking you for money, so much so that you feel like an ATM. You develop a fear of not having enough money (yes, just like the rest of us!). And you are burdened by not knowing how best to steward your money—what investments to make, what organizations to give to, etc.

Most of us imagine that if we had a lot more money, our problems would disappear. Will reminded us that while money solves a lot of problems, it introduces others.

The real challenge, whether we've got a lot or a little, is one of stewardship. Will we use the money God has given us faithfully for the sake of others? Will we walk down the path of justice, learning to thrive as we equip others to thrive? Or will we muddle along on our own path?

MONEY IS NOT UNJUST . . . BUT IT CAN BE USED UNJUSTLY

Here's another startling truism about money: It's not inherently evil. That's right, there is nothing in the Bible that says money (having money, spending money, making money) is bad.

There are many examples in the Bible of wealthy people who loved and followed God and were examples of deep faith—Abraham, Isaac, Joseph, David, Solomon, Job. Some of the women who followed Jesus were wealthy enough to fund his ministry and that of the other disciples (see Luke 8:1–3).

When the Apostle Paul addresses those with wealth, he doesn't simply say, "It's bad for you to have money. Give it all away." He commands the wealthy "not to be haughty, nor to set their hopes on the uncertainty of riches, but on God, who richly provides us with everything to enjoy" (1 Timothy 6:17). Did you catch that? What God gives to us we are allowed to enjoy. But there is a balance here. The rich are also expected "to do good, to be rich in good works, to be generous and ready to share" (1 Timothy 6:18). Apparently, those with money are allowed to enjoy its benefits, but not in such a way that there is no room for generosity.

There's also nothing wrong with profit and working hard to seek profit. Businesses have to have profit in order to survive and thrive. You can't provide jobs, hire employees, offer goods and services, or spur on economies without profit.

The Book of Proverbs often speaks encouragingly about profit-making. For instance, this proverb about the benefit of work: "In all toil there is profit, but mere talk tends only to poverty" (Proverbs 14:23).

Or this proverb about planning ahead: "Go to the ant, O sluggard, and consider her ways . . . she prepares her bread in summer and gathers her food in harvest" (Proverbs 6:6, 8).

Or this proverb about building wealth and passing that wealth to the next generation: "A good man leaves an inheritance to his children's children" (Proverbs 13:22).

Biblically speaking, neither having money nor making money are inherently unjust. And yet, as we all know, so much injustice centers around money. Why? Because we love it, we want to have it, we believe we need more of it, we feel like it's ours, and we want the things it provides.

Many of us believe money will save us. We don't usually put it in those terms, but deep down, we think, *If only we had more money, everything would be better.*

No wonder Paul warned, not about *money*, but about the *love of money*: "For the love of money is a root of all kinds of evil. Some people, eager for money, have wandered from the faith and pierced themselves with many griefs" (1 Timothy 6:10, NIV).

It's not hard to see many of the "griefs" the love of money has produced in our society. The love of money manifests in side deals within "good ole boy" networks, shutting out others. It manifests in the lottery, which essentially taxes the poorest in our communities. It manifests in payday lending companies, preying on those in desperate need. It manifests in astronomical interest rates for those with little credit history—usually those living in poverty.

Money is not inherently unjust, but as a tangible form of power, it can be used for justice or injustice. Like all power, it tends to multiply. Those with a lot of money find it easier to get more money.

There's a danger here. The more we get money, the more it "gets" us. Money has the power to rule over us and others. This is why Jesus said it was impossible to serve God and money. We think all we're doing is collecting assets. But really, we're rooting our hearts somewhere. And we can only root our hearts in one soil. Will it be the soil of God or the soil of wealth?

Once again, we return to the question of stewardship. Will we use the money God has given us faithfully? Will we walk down the path of justice, learning to thrive as we equip others to thrive?

Fortunately for us, the Bible doesn't leave us in the dark here. It provides some principles for stewarding the power we have with money. I see three main principles:

PRINCIPLE 1: GLEANING

In the Old Testament law, God gave this command to his people:

> "When you reap the harvest of your land, you shall not reap your field right up to its edge, neither shall you gather the gleanings after your harvest. And you shall not strip your vineyard bare, neither shall you gather the fallen grapes of your vineyard. You shall leave them for the poor and for the sojourner: I am the Lord your God." (Leviticus 19:9–10)

This "gleaning" law allowed poor people to provide for themselves without relying on benevolence. They were not just given food; they were also given the dignity of work.

In an agrarian society, the application here is pretty straightforward. But very few of us are farmers—and even if we were, with technological changes, we probably wouldn't apply this principle the same way. So what's the principle? I'd put it like this: Do not take all of the profits; leave some margin so people have the opportunity to work with dignity to provide for themselves.

What might this look like today? It may simply be paying higher wages within your company rather than paying the lowest amount your industry allows. It may mean offering ownership opportunities to your employees. Or it might mean setting aside profit to offer additional jobs or to invest in the community. Maybe you decide to eliminate negotiation—a keystone element of maximizing profit—instead opting for a transparent cost approach. Or perhaps you place a cap on executive-level salaries.

These are just a few ideas. I bet you can come up with another dozen. Start with the principle—leave some profit on the margin for the sake of others—and see where the Spirit leads.

PRINCIPLE 2: JUBILEE

Later in the Book of Leviticus, there's an interesting account of a little-known holy day called "Jubilee." Here's the account:

> The Lord spoke to Moses on Mount Sinai, saying, "Speak to the people of Israel and say to them, When you come into the land that I give you, the land shall keep a Sabbath to the Lord. For six years you shall sow your field, and for six years you shall prune your vineyard and gather in its fruits, but in the seventh year there shall be a Sabbath of solemn rest for the land, a Sabbath to the Lord. You shall not sow your field or prune your vineyard. You shall not reap what grows of itself in your harvest,

or gather the grapes of your undressed vine. It shall be a year of solemn rest for the land. The Sabbath of the land shall provide food for you, for yourself and for your male and female slaves and for your hired worker and the sojourner who lives with you, and for your cattle and for the wild animals that are in your land: all its yield shall be for food.

You shall count seven weeks of years, seven times seven years, so that the time of the seven weeks of years shall give you forty-nine years. Then you shall sound the loud trumpet on the tenth day of the seventh month. On the Day of Atonement you shall sound the trumpet throughout all your land. And you shall consecrate the fiftieth year, and proclaim liberty throughout the land to all its inhabitants. It shall be a jubilee for you, when each of you shall return to his property and each of you shall return to his clan. That fiftieth year shall be a jubilee for you; in it you shall neither sow nor reap what grows of itself nor gather the grapes from the undressed vines. For it is a jubilee. It shall be holy to you. You may eat the produce of the field. (Leviticus 25:1–12)

Jubilee follows the principle of the Sabbath, but on a much larger scale. The Sabbath, you'll recall, was one day out of every seven when the people did not work. Here God extends that to the annual level: Every seventh year was a "year of Sabbath," when debts were canceled and slaves were set free.

That's exciting enough. But Jubilee wasn't every seven years. It was every seven sevens—every forty-nine years. On a Jubilee year, the land would go back to the original owners. This was a once-in-a-lifetime chance to start afresh, no matter how irresponsible a person or a family had been.

It's hard to imagine anything like this in our world today. But even though we won't likely be able to create a Jubilee Year in the United States (or even in North Carolina . . . or Raleigh . . . or my neighborhood!), I think we can apply some of the Jubilee principles in our spheres of influence.

Here are a few principles from Jubilee that just leaders should apply:

- God owns everything; it's all his, not ours.
- Our money and possessions do not save us, so we can be free to give them to others.
- We live in a "we" society, not a "me" society. Therefore, others have a right to my stuff, and it's not right for me to withhold it from them.
- Injustice needs to be resolved, whether people have been responsible or not.
- Some debts just need to be forgiven.

Again, I bet you can come up with some other ways to practice Jubilee. Maybe you carve out space for sabbatical time for your employees. Or you budget a certain amount of your profit specifically to forgive debts.

Get creative about this. Dream a bit about what it might look like to give away Jubilee.

PRINCIPLE 3: RADICAL GENEROSITY

Remember what Zacchaeus said after Jesus invited himself over for a meal at his house?

> And Zacchaeus stood and said to the Lord, "Behold, Lord, the half of my goods I give to the poor. And if I have defrauded anyone of anything, I restore it fourfold." And Jesus said to him, "Today salvation has come to this house, since he also is a son of Abraham. For the Son of Man came to seek and to save the lost." (Luke 19:8–10)

The law required that Zacchaeus pay back 120 percent of what he had defrauded (see Leviticus 6:2–5). Zacchaeus opted to pay back 400 percent. The law required people to give away 10 percent of their money. Zacchaeus offered to give away 50 percent. *That's radical generosity.*

What does it mean for us to be radically generous? I'm not going to give you any numbers to shoot for. In the Bible, offerings are all over the place. Some people, apparently, gave everything they owned. Others didn't. But one thing is consistent: As with Zacchaeus, people who met Jesus gave in ways we could only define as *radical*.

This may feel a bit subjective. But ask the Spirit to guide you. Pray, "God, how do you want me to steward my money for peace and justice?" Ask him to guide you, like Zacchaeus, who gave radically out of the realization that Jesus saved him. He was safe, secure. Money was not what he needed to be whole. Jesus made him whole. And he responded.

IS IT OK TO . . . ?

I want to end this chapter by addressing some questions that may have popped into your mind as you have been reading it. Questions like *Can I have too much wealth? Is it OK to live in a large home—or to have multiple homes? Is it wrong to join a country club? How do we think about the schools we send our children to? Should I feel guilty for buying nice things or going on expensive vacations?*

I realize that I may start to step on some toes here. And I want to acknowledge up front that it matters much more that you follow 1) the leading of the Spirit and 2) the principles of Scripture than that you take my advice here as infallible truth. That said, I think there is some benefit to making this incredibly practical. My goal is to help you ask *justice* questions about your wealth. Remember: the path to justice and the path to thriving are the same path.

Deep breath. Let's get into it.

1. Can someone have too much wealth?

The answer is no! There is no line of wealth or possessions that makes a person just or unjust. Poverty isn't a virtue. Wealth isn't a vice. It's what you *do* with what you have that matters. Are you stewarding it in a way that allows you to have open hands? Or are you so consumed with getting more money that money has "gotten" you?

Here are some indications that wealth is "getting" you:

- Your success equals your value.
- You believe what you have will satisfy you.
- You believe you've earned everything you have, instead of seeing your wealth (and skills) as gifts from God.
- You're isolated from people in material need and have no relationships with them.
- You always want more.
- You're stingy with your money and possessions.
- You're physically unhealthy.
- You don't sleep well.
- Your relationships with your family are mediocre.
- You have no one in your life who speaks truth to you.
- You have no trusting relationships with people from a different culture or background.
- You feel a decent amount of stress and anxiety.
- You're unaware of the brokenness people are experiencing around you.
- You're disengaged from a local church community.

Notice how none of those questions are about the number you claim on your tax returns!

2. If you have a big home (or multiple homes), how can you be a just leader?

As it is with income, so it is with your home: There isn't a "just" square-footage above which you automatically enter the realm of injustice. Personally, I have been embarrassed that my home is both too big (when having certain people over) and too small (when others come over).

Here are some thoughts to help you think about stewarding your home toward justice:

- Use your home as a place to welcome all kinds of people.
- Make others feel like it's their home as much as it is yours.
- When there is a need, let people stay with you.
- Don't worry about the way it looks to others.
- Steward your home well. Take care of it, pay down the mortgage, and consider ways to save to free up resources for others.

3. Can just leaders be members of a country club? If so, what would that look like?

To be honest, this is a tough one for me. I grew up learning how to play golf from my grandfather at the country club in Jackson, Mississippi, where he was a member. It was the 1970s, so the community was steeped in racial prejudice and violence. The club typified a lot of that prejudice, not allowing people of color to join or use the course. Over the years, like many other country clubs, it has been reluctant (though not completely resistant) to allow different groups of people to become members.

How is it possible for an institution to be like that and its members to be just?

Many just leaders will decide that they don't want to engage in the country club world. I respect that. But for those who are in that world, here are some ways you can steward this complicated institution toward justice:

- Build trusting relationships with other members.
- Redeem its history (if it needs redemption). Start by learning about the founding and the values that drove the club. See if it may have restricted membership for certain types of people or engaged in other unjust practices. Work with the leadership to challenge and address any restrictions that may still exist.
- Open up opportunities for different types of people to become members or have greater access.

- Push the club and its members to use their resources to empower and elevate those in material need in the community.
- Make sure that club employees are paid well and are able to grow.

4. What about where we choose to send our children to school? Public, private, homeschool, charter? Is one decision more just than another?

Whew, this decision is top of mind for most every parent—at least for those who feel like they have a choice. Some parents don't, either because of finances, location, or transportation challenges. But for those of us who have the ability to choose, this is a legitimately tough decision. Most of us want what is best for our children regarding their education, and there are many factors to consider. Which ones help us be just?

Full disclosure: Even though I went to an elite, private middle and high school, my wife and I have been deeply committed to public schools. All of our children went to and graduated from public schools. We made this choice because we believed they would not only get a good education, but a great one. More importantly, we felt they would have the opportunity to build peer relationships with diverse groups of people, something that has been critical for their future.

Again, that was our choice. It's not the only path for just leaders. Parents (and ultimately their children) can pursue justice from any educational environment—private or public, Christian, homeschool, or anything else. The question is, *How do we steward our education for God's peace and justice?*

Each environment requires us to take intentional steps to pursue justice. Let's consider a few.

If your children are at private schools, here are some things to consider:

- Learn its history—and, if needed, redeem its history. As with many country clubs, so it is with many private schools: Their founding may have been the result of injustice or may have excluded certain groups. Even if previous restrictions were removed, it's possible barriers still exist for many groups. Do your homework so you can help change the narrative.

- Seek regular opportunities for your kids to develop peer relationships with people who have a different background from them or have material needs. This will likely be tough if there is little ethnic and economic diversity in their school environment. But it is very important to expose your kids to diverse groups of people—and not just to serve them but build peer friendships with them—to help your kids develop the skill and empathy to cross cultural barriers.

- Help them navigate the pressure they face to perform, achieve, and meet everyone's expectations. Kids are under serious pressure. That pressure is usually elevated in a private environment, where achievement is expected and getting into a great college is the goal.

- Give them a vision for stewarding their education to provide peace and justice to those around them, using what they learn and experience for others, not just themselves.

- Take meaningful steps to ensure the school can welcome and equip students of all different backgrounds.

If your children are at Christian schools:

- Start with the history. Many Christian schools in the South, for instance, began as a reaction to the integration efforts of the Civil Rights Movement. Nearly one-third of the schools within the Association of Christian Schools International (ACSI), the largest non-Catholic Christian school association in the United States, were established shortly before or after the U.S. Supreme Court mandated public school desegregation, when many White families fled the public school system. They often struggle to diversify their student bodies today. In September 2019, more than half of all ACSI member schools, which account for about 45 percent of all non-Catholic Christian schools in the United States, reported that 80 percent or more of their students are White.[65] Once again, it's important to do our homework.

- Make sure your children have the opportunity to develop peer relationships with people who are not like them—across faith, race, and other differences. Choose sports leagues, camps, theater and art programs, even playgrounds where children are different. Go regularly. Make friends. Take intentional steps to be with people and in places where people are different from you and make them a part of your normal routine.

- Help the school pursue diversity without requiring minority groups to have to assimilate. There are very few models of this, since many private Christian schools (though certainly not all) are mostly made up of well-resourced White families and students. The resulting culture and way of doing things favors that demographic. Students from other backgrounds end up having to assimilate to that culture and give up parts of who they are when they attend the school. Private Christian schools can offset this by:
  - Believing at the leadership levels that ethnic and cultural diversity is foundational to the life and health of the school
  - Pursuing strategies that engage and lift up people from different cultures and backgrounds
  - Building a team of diverse leaders and teachers
  - Using curriculum that celebrates and studies leaders, authors, and experts of color
  - Being creative with the ways the school is funded and providing opportunities for children to attend from families with different economic backgrounds
  - Building relationships with diverse leaders in the community to learn how the school can be an empowering place of education for all students in the community

- Being willing to make small meaningful changes over the long haul, knowing it will take time to see meaningful results

A Christian school, founded on the principles of a just God, should feel some discomfort if that school is predominantly White and only accessible by people of wealth. Schools like this should look in the mirror and ask, "How can we be just?" That's not an easy question to answer, and there are many ways to tackle it. But the first step is to ask the question.

If your children are at public schools:

- Help them navigate the ways they think about faith as they are presented with a variety of different ideologies and truths. Take intentional steps to ensure they can build a biblical worldview that does not judge, but rather enables them to love others and winsomely talk about God's truth.
- Encourage them to build relationships with people who are different from them. Even though they likely will be around many people with different backgrounds, most kids gravitate to people like themselves. Challenge your kids to cross the divides. For yourself, build relationships with parents of different backgrounds to help make those connections with your children.
- Invest in the leadership and the teachers. Find ways to give them capacity. Join the PTA—yes, even us dads. I served one year as the PTA president at our children's high school. Alice, my wife, served multiple years as president at our children's elementary, middle, and high schools. Many PTAs are working with limited resources and need the support and time of committed parents.
- Advocate for helpful changes, not just at your school level, but at the system level. Many public school systems have policies that need to be changed to make things more just and equitable for everyone. Find out what you can do to be a part of those changes.

The educational choices for our kids are complex, nuanced, and child-specific, requiring real thought and prayer. In every environment, we have to remember: *What is normal may not be just.* It takes being willing to step out, even to rock the boat, for us to steward our children's education for God's peace and justice. It's not always the easiest path to walk, but it's always worth it.

5. Do just leaders buy nice things and enjoy nice vacations?

By this point, I'm hoping you know where I'm headed with this. Yes, you can buy nice things. Enjoy them, too. Yes, you can go on a nice vacation. Don't feel guilty about it.

That said, the goal of life is not to get more cool stuff and more awesome experiences. Be mindful, remembering that the most satisfying use of your wealth is not for you to have more fun, but to multiply more joy around you.

Whether it's new toys or a fancy vacation, here are a few questions just leaders may want to consider:

- Do we really need to spend this amount of money for this purchase or vacation? Are there ways to save and still have a great experience?
- Who can enjoy this with us?
- What if we gave this away to someone who really needs it?

NOT LESS WEALTHY, BUT DIFFERENTLY WEALTHY

You may not be as wealthy as my friend Will. Then again, you might have ten times the money he does. Either way, my guess is that you've got enough money to ask the questions we've considered in this chapter. It may take you a while to land on answers you can really own. That's fine. Keep asking the questions, using your creative energy to dream about what gleaning, Jubilee, and radical generosity might look like in your context.

And remember: In God's economy, what we give away isn't lost in some zero-sum calculation. God's approach to wealth isn't necessarily meant to make you less wealthy, but *differently* wealthy. It allows you to use money without letting money use you. It allows you to experience true flourishing while you multiply flourishing in the lives of others.

It allows you to taste the fruits of justice—and plant seeds for others to taste it, too.

Just leaders allow God to transform their view of power, their view of work, their view of money. And, as we're about to see . . . their view of success.

QUESTIONS TO CONSIDER

1. How do you feel about money? Do you think about it often? Rarely?

2. Does talking about money leave you feeling guilty or ashamed? Or proud and confident?

3. What about the money you have? Do you feel like you have enough? Do you wish you had more?

4. Do you hold on to your money? Do you find yourself being stingy? Or do you hold your money loosely and feel free to be generous with your money?

5. What steps do you need to take to be free from the love of money and be wildly generous?

CHAPTER 16

Power and Success

What is success for you? How would you define it? If you're struggling to come up with a definition, jump in your imaginary time machine. Fast forward ten, twenty, or thirty years. As you step out of your time machine, someone tells you, "This is your future. You've done everything you dreamed. You've made it." That future dream? *That's* your definition of success.

For me, growing up, success was pretty simple: *Win.* Win the game. Win the test. Win the award. Win the job.

Fortunately, winning wasn't the *only* thing on my mind. But when I thought about success, there was only one rubric: Win. Be the best. Achieve excellence. Stand out.

I'm not alone in this. As *New York Times* columnist David Brooks argues in his book *The Second Mountain*,[66] most of us arrange our lives around climbing the mountain of achievement. Some of us make it to the summit. Others of us don't. But there is little discussion about whether we should be scaling the mountain at all. It's just assumed.

For just leaders, there is—to borrow Brooks's metaphor—a second, more significant mountain. Success is not about *less* than achievement. But it becomes about much *more* as well. It is deeper, richer, more complete. In this vision of success, achievement and prospering are still the goal (the "righteous prospering" of Proverbs 11:10) but the motivation is quite different (the "city rejoicing").

If the whole city rejoices because you are prospering, then what does your success need to look like? Why would everyone in the city, from the poorest of the poor to the richest of the rich, dance wildly in the streets because *you* are winning?

	SUCCESS AS **WINNING**	SUCCESS AS **FLOURISHING**
FOCUS	Individual	Communal
OUTCOME	Winning (Win-Lose)	Equity (Win-Win)
MOTIVATION	Competitive	Restorative

OPTION 1: SUCCESS-AS-WINNING

If we're going to answer those questions, we must take the time to redefine success. Let's look, first, at how success is normally defined. I'm calling this the "success-as-winning" model. What are the key elements of this vision of success?

First, success is mostly *individual*. It's mostly about me.

"I love me some me!" The Hall of Fame NFL receiver Terrell Owens, famously coined that phrase during a game as a member of the Philadelphia Eagles. Brash, confident, and extraordinarily talented, he enthusiastically exclaimed how proud he was of himself and all he had accomplished.

We may not be as overt in our praise of self as Owens. But we probably recognize something of ourselves in that statement.

We love individual success. It's why sports talk shows spend hours *ad nauseum* debating who's the GOAT—the "greatest of all time." Who's the best basketball player of all time—Michael Jordan or LeBron James? The best quarterback—Tom Brady or Joe Montana? The best women's tennis player—no debate; it's Serena. The best men's tennis player—Roger Federer, Rafael Nadal, or Novak Djokovic?

It's not just in sports, either. We're *always* on the lookout for the

MVP: the most outstanding student, the Oscar winner, the number-one Billboard artist, the national merit semifinalist, the scholarship winner.

Second, success-as-winning is about *meeting our own needs*. This makes complete sense if success is primarily individual. My goal is to make something of myself. But that can only happen if I'm comfortable and taken care of. So the "good life" I imagine for myself is mainly about meeting my needs—or, often, meeting desires I've justified as "needs," even if they aren't really necessary.

We want to have more money, more friends, more toys, and more security. Success seems like the natural way to get them. We want people to like us and find value in what we do, and we want to achieve so we can have more control over our lives and do what we want when we want.

In short, we want to win because we want more power.

Finally, success-as-winning is inherently *competitive*. Somebody wins, and somebody loses. Prestige, accomplishment, the highest score. If I win, then you lose. And it puts us in direct comparison to others. With success-as-winning, it doesn't matter if I've done something impressive, helpful, or praiseworthy. It only matters that what I've done is *more* impressive, *more* helpful, *more* praiseworthy than others.

This is why so many of us feel so terrible when we look at social media (and it's why I've had to limit my use of it). As much as I enjoy scrolling through Instagram and Facebook to see the pictures and videos of "my friends," I often close the apps with a profound feeling of discontentment. I'd feel bitter seeing how much fun everyone appeared to be having, how good they looked, or how smart they were. There they are, going on a nice vacation or starting some exciting new business or buying a new car, and I'm just watching it all on my phone while I wait in line at the grocery. Instead of being excited for them, I'd resent them. In my mind, they were winning, and I was losing. No fun.

OPTION 2: SUCCESS-AS-FLOURISHING

True success isn't simply the opposite of success-as-winning. There are still elements of caring for yourself and engaging in healthy competition. But true success adds another dimension. I'm calling it "success-as-flourishing," because the bottom line is bigger than personal power. It's about rejoicing, flourishing, wholeness. It's about the entire city dancing in the streets.

What does our success need to look like in order for the whole city to rejoice?

First, instead of only being individual, success-as-flourishing is also communal. My success is incomplete until it is found in others' success. I don't win unless you do, too, and my success leads to your success.

Alice and I experienced this firsthand when we bravely signed up to run a Tough Mudder race with our close friends Erik and Kelly. What is a Tough Mudder, you ask? It's a military style obstacle course race filled with a variety of challenges—and mountains of mud. You race as a team, and you win as a team. If you go it alone, not only will you lose, but you could actually get hurt. Everyone needs everyone else to get through the course. But here's what's interesting. Halfway through the course, teams realize they don't just need their teammates to get through the course—they need other teams, too. So, everyone begins to help one another. We could not get over a barrier without another team's help, and then once we got to the top, we helped the next team. All of a sudden, it was about everyone finishing. If we all finished, we all won.

I can't tell you how satisfying it was to get to the end of the race. We were covered in mud, completely exhausted, and high-fiving random people all around us. Everyone had officially become Tough Mudders!

That's what communal success should be. We are all wildly celebrating when others around us win. What *I* do makes *you* rejoice, and what *you* do makes *me* rejoice. Even if we're completely filthy.

What does this look like outside of a Tough Mudder race? What's required for our success to be truly communal?

We are known in relationship with one another. We can't be isolated. We have to be engaged with and connected to one another.

We must love our neighbor—know them and care for them. Have them know us. We get to love those who are hurting, understand their needs, and build trust with them. We even need to love our enemies and be people who care for those others discard.

Success-as-flourishing requires that people feel a part of the city. They have a sense of real community, of pride in the place where they live and work and shop. The people belong to the place and to one another.

We make decisions with everyone in mind. Not just those in our organization. Not just our stakeholders. Not just people who understand what our organization does. But everyone who might be impacted by what we're doing.

Second, instead of being solely competitive (win/lose), success-as-flourishing aims to be *equitable* (win/win).

Frankly, this is hard for many of us to imagine. Win/win examples are inspiring, but they're rare. But I don't believe they need to *stay* rare. I believe that with the right creative energy, we can succeed in ways that not only benefit us but also benefit others. Rather than competing for slices of a pie, we can grow the pie.

Equity never happens by accident. It needs to be pursued if it's ever going to be achieved.

One way we pursue equity is by sharing resources. As with money, we recognize that what we have is not our own, and others have a right to it. We consider how to be extravagantly generous and sacrifice. We may be generous with our money. But we can also be generous with our personnel, our time, and our wisdom.

The goal of equity isn't to bring everyone *down* to the same level. It's to bring everyone up. In a truly equitable environment, people are elevated, and we help them have access to resources and opportunities they haven't had before.

Third, instead of simply meeting our needs, success-as-flourishing is *restorative* (meets everyone's needs). Brokenness is restored; oppression is gone. People are secure and living out what they are designed to be. There is growth, life, health, and beauty. People are worshiping and glorifying God.

Practically, let's see what this looks like.

AM I USING MY SUCCESS FOR JUSTICE?

Let's consider what questions we need to ask ourselves to determine whether we are being just in our pursuit of success.

How do I know I am operating out of the success-as-flourishing mindset? To put it another way, *Am I using my success for justice?*

Ask yourself:

- Am I placing my faith in God and depending upon him?
- Am I showing love toward my spouse and my children?
- Have I listened to and understood the needs of the people around me?
- Am I helping others to utilize their strengths and pursue opportunities to grow?
- Am I helping people in material need or hurting them? Are they rejoicing?
- Am I learning the story of the systems I'm part of?
- Am I honoring the history of a community?
- Am I fostering relationships and community, particularly across cultural, economic, and other social divides?
- Am I creating opportunities for people to work and provide for themselves and their families?
- Am I setting aside some of the profits to give opportunities for people to thrive?
- Am I including marginalized voices to come up with and provide solutions? Do they have a seat at the table?

- Am I creating wealth for those who are materially poor and underserved?
- Am I giving power away?
- Am I including others in conversations about justice? Am I OK to risk my network to move people in that direction?

Success-as-flourishing is comprehensive, others-centered, and pushes us into areas where we are uncomfortable. It forces us to consider the needs of others before our own and seek the welfare of those in our communities who are hurting and broken.

Now, you may say, *This sounds idealistic and wonderful, but it isn't realistic.*

Fair point, and in many ways, you are right. Not *every* decision or action will fit with all the questions above. It's not possible to consider the totality of what it means to be just all the time. And that's OK. Some of this will be relevant, and some of it won't. But I hope you get the idea. We are taking the themes and concepts we have covered in the book and using them to evaluate success differently. We don't want justice to be something we do; we want it to be who we *are*—part of our DNA.

To which you might say (this time with a bit of an exhausted sigh), *David, I need to pursue profit. I need to be competitive. My business lives in a world that doesn't operate according to your principles. I just couldn't operate like this and actually stay in business.*

And I would say you are right again . . . sort of.

STAYING COMPETITIVE *AND* BEING JUST

I'll admit it: Sometimes doing the just thing seems in conflict with what will help the leader or organization stay competitive and be successful. And as much as you'd *like* to pursue justice, you know you *need* to keep the lights on.

For instance, here are some real tensions you may face:

- Choosing to earn less profit on a project to give opportunities to others but yielding less return to investors
- Spending time learning about the history of your community, your vendors, your networks—time that you could be investing in growing your business
- Hiring someone from a different background/culture who will need more time to learn the cultural norms of your business to become a meaningful producer
- Paying higher wages and offering better benefits (giving employees time to rest) which cut into profits

These tensions are real. They might intimidate many people into throwing up their hands and giving up. But have you gotten to your current position by giving up every time you've encountered a challenge? Is that your usual response to difficulty? *Ah, seems tough . . . I should probably give up.*

I doubt it.

You climbed a ladder to achieve your current leadership role. You brought your "A game." You exercised grit and intelligence and creativity. What I'm asking you to do is to reach into that resource bag of yours and *do it again.* Being just *and* competitive at the same time is a challenge. But you're not allergic to challenge. It's time to step up your leadership.

Are you content to be an OK leader, middling around after your own bottom line? Or do you want to be a just leader, a world-class leader with a broad view of success? I don't think you'd have made it to this point in the book if you were the former. Now is the time to elevate your perspective and vision of what it means to be a leader.

Here are five ways you can elevate your perspective to pursue justice and stay competitive:

1. To pursue justice *and* stay competitive, just leaders must look for and implement operational efficiencies. Margins may be lower because of the desire to be equitable and generous, so costs must be maintained through highly efficient operational practices. Just leaders are keenly aware of how their business works and can identify inefficiencies that are costing too much time and money. They address those inefficiencies, improve processes, and constantly learn about and look for best practices.

2. To pursue justice *and* stay competitive, just leaders are excellent communicators. They have the unique ability to cast vision to investors even if returns may be lower than in other investments. They set the right expectations for vendors and other stakeholders. They deliver high value to customers. They do what they say they're going to do. They effectively handle conflict, addressing it head on, with the right balance of gentleness and firmness.

3. To pursue justice *and* stay competitive, just leaders invest in their people. They make sure to put the right people in the right positions. They are not afraid to make hard decisions to move people into those positions and care for those who may need to leave. They give clear expectations to their employees so they know their roles and how their work fits in the overall business. They give their people the tools they need to be successful and hold them accountable. They reward them, affirm them, help them see how they can grow, and encourage their health and rest.

4. To pursue justice *and* stay competitive, just leaders are constantly innovative and creative. They are constantly improving, looking out for the latest trends and upcoming markets, and willing to take (informed!) risks.

5. To pursue justice *and* stay competitive, just leaders stay generous. They are willing to share their profits and ownership with their people. They limit their salaries to free up extra resources to provide opportunities to others. They are deeply connected in their community to ensure the work they are doing is causing the whole city to rejoice.

Jump in your imaginary time machine one more time. Fast-forward to the end of your career. As you step out of your time machine, someone tells you, "This is your future. You've done everything you dreamed. *You've made it.*" Wouldn't you like to be looking around at a flourishing, joyful community, one that you helped to build?

It doesn't have to be a dream. With the right actions today, we can make that dream a reality. It's time to consider what bold, courageous action looks like.

QUESTIONS TO CONSIDER

1. In what ways have you believed success is about winning?
2. What can success-as-flourishing begin to look like for you and those you lead?
3. What steps do you need to take to be more just and still remain competitive?
4. What would you do in a situation where you can't be both competitive and just at the same time?

QUALITY 4

Take Bold, Courageous Action

Throughout this book, I have provided steps for you to take to be a just leader who fills the community with joy. Instead of waiting until *this* section to talk about what steps to take, I've wanted to help you see that being just is about who we are, not just what we do. If we are just at the very core of our being, then it is natural that we would take action in every aspect of our lives. Justice would be in our DNA.

It's as if I am giving you a new pair of glasses through which you now see the world. With those glasses, you recognize things you may not have recognized before. You understand the best ways to engage injustice around you and act justly. Hopefully, that kind of vision will become normal to you. You won't have to "put the glasses on" as intentionally or as often. You'll just see differently. You won't be thinking, "OK, time to pursue some justice." You simply will *be*.

But let's be honest: Few of us have reached that stage yet. We need more training wheels to help us become people of justice. Especially for those of us who have rarely considered ideas surrounding justice, we need a nudge toward action. If all we ever do is talk about justice, something has gone wrong.

Just leaders act. They step in. They do not—in fact, *cannot*—sit idly by when something is unjust. They don't always know the best solutions. But they know they can't do nothing.

Does that frighten you a bit? I know it unnerves me. After all, for those of us who have power and who live in a world designed for us, *taking action is optional*. If I see and am aware of injustice, that injustice rarely is directed toward me. So I don't really have to do anything. I can keep going about my life and not have to deal with outside social pressures to engage issues of justice. Because whether I act or not, not much is going to change with my life.

I also recognize that when injustice happens, I am not the one who bears a cost. And that can be really frustrating for those who do bear the cost. When I am apathetic, disinterested, or critical of those who are raising the banner of justice, I can become insensitive and insulting without even knowing it.

Even writing this book—putting myself on record, publicly stating that *I am someone who wants to pursue justice*—can feel disingenuous for me. I don't truly know injustice. I don't experience it on a regular basis. I hardly know what it takes to overcome injustice. Nor do I understand the cost.

Am I trying to understand? To listen? To see? Absolutely. But there's a world of difference between trying to enter into injustice and feeling it, experiencing it, living it.

When victims of injustice put their trust in people who have power and are met with disdain and apathy, they bear a tremendous cost—a cost I cannot begin to understand.

And so, just leaders are people who recognize taking action is not optional. But it will require us to be bold and courageous.

Bold—because many actions will require real faith, stepping out of our comfort zone and going against the norm, and possibly doing something we have never done before.

Bold does not necessarily mean *extraordinary* or *amazing* or *life-transforming*—words we like to use to puff ourselves up. In fact, being bold is often quite the opposite. Most bold actions are patently ordinary—everyday, small, faithful steps fueled by a conviction to bring healing to a fractured community.

What makes an action bold isn't the *grandness* of the action, but the *discomfort* of it. No one ever changed the world being comfortable. If you're comfortable, you might have to check whether you are being just or not. Typically, the path of least resistance is the wrong path to take.

And courageous—because you will face obstacles along the way. You will need courage. Courage to stand your ground, courage to say hard things, courage to confront conflict and even attacks from people close to you, and courage to stay in the game when it seems no progress is being made.

Just leaders often have to use a different grid to determine whether the steps they are taking are right or not. They often are going against the grain. So how do you know whether you're doing what is just or not?

Let's take a look at three helpful tests. Bold and courageous action is 1) unpopular, 2) disruptive, and 3) slow.

CHAPTER 17

Action That's Unpopular

Tyler got a call from one of his customers. She needed help. As the CEO of a commercial pressure washing company, Tyler and his team had built a strong business and a great reputation in the community. Tyler was used to receiving all kinds of calls. Calls of praise. Calls of frustration and complaint. But this call was a bit different.

After multiple incidents of police shootings of Black men across the country, a group of people had gone out to a parking lot and painted the names of victims of police brutality. Technically, this was vandalism, though it was clear the goal was simply to honor those who had been victims.

The trouble was, people driving vehicles to that parking lot the next day did not want to park in the parking spaces with those names. Some people were upset that the names were there at all. Others appreciated it, but they did not want to dishonor the people named by driving their cars on top of them and parking in the spaces.

The upshot for the property manager, though, was that overnight, the shopping center's parking capacity had effectively been cut in half. And that was bad for business. She was not necessarily disagreeing with the sentiment of what the group did, but the shopping center was losing customers. People were turning around and going elsewhere to shop. She could not have half of her parking lot made unavailable.

This is when she called Tyler. Could he have a crew come out and clean the parking lot?

But there was a problem. Most of the crews at Tyler's business consisted of Black men. They felt the pain of the recent shootings and internalized the reality that they (or those they love) could be targeted in a similar way. How would they feel washing off the drawings of those who had been killed?

Tyler was stuck. On one hand, he felt a responsibility to meet the needs, desires, and expectations of his customer. On the other hand, he felt a responsibility to be sensitive to the feelings and needs of his employees.

What should he do?

As we have mentioned before, doing the just thing is often in conflict with what may be profitable or what meets the needs of our customers. When that happens, decisions aren't usually straightforward. Leaders have to operate in gray areas and make decisions without complete confidence in the outcome.

When this happens, many leaders are aided by popular opinion to help them decide what to do. They rightly seek outside counsel to help them navigate the factors that go into their decision and direct their thinking. And they often choose what most people affirm—in other words, what's most popular. Sometimes—rarely, I think—that's appropriate and helpful. But more often than not, it's toxic.

Just leaders can't simply rely on popular opinion to give them confidence to act.

If we live in an unjust world, we need to acknowledge that "just" and "normal" don't always live in the same sphere. Unfortunately, we have often gotten so used to "normal" that it can be hard for us to register injustice.

For instance, in chapter 10 we saw that 38,000,000 Americans live in poverty. That's normal. Many of us just accept it. But it's not just.

Or consider the vast difference between secondary schools throughout our country. Even if I limit myself to the public schools within my county, there is a huge disparity between the resources from one school to another. That's normal, but it's not just.

Or what about our hiring practices? The path of least resistance is to hire people like us, from within our networks. That's normal, but it's not necessarily just.

It's normal for us to focus solely on our bottom line, to keep our power for ourselves, to keep a tight grip on our money. But that's not the way of Jesus. And if it's not the way of Jesus, it's not just.

The actions of just leaders go against the grain and are inherently unpopular. That's why we are so hesitant to act. I'm not sure about you, but I don't like not being liked. So I will try to rationalize not doing anything. Or I'll take a very small step that hardly requires anything from me at all—just to say I did something.

But just leaders can't let others' opinions hold them back. Remember, we are already justified—the Lord has shown us what it looks like to be just, and our position with him is secure! We don't need popular opinion any more to prop us up. We are freed up to focus, instead, on what is good, right, and just.

Even if it means we need to 1) go it alone, 2) be misunderstood, and 3) face criticism.

GO IT ALONE

If what you do is not popular, you can expect to feel and be alone. Ironically, if you feel that way, you aren't alone!

Jesus, the ultimate just leader and *tsaddiqim*, often forged ahead without other people understanding what he was doing. By the end, all twelve of his disciples had abandoned him. One had betrayed him. His top disciple, Peter, denied he had even met him. And as he died on a cross, Jesus cried out, "My God, my God, why have you forsaken me?" (Matthew 27:46). He was utterly alone.

We'll never experience that level of separation and isolation. But if we're living as just leaders, we should prepare for our share of it.

Now, I want to be clear here. I'm not saying you need to be a renegade and throw all caution to the wind, blowing up everything around you that you feel is unjust. I'm also not saying that *if* you're standing alone, *then* you must be in the right. It's possible to be flying solo and still be in the wrong. You need wisdom, discernment, and counsel from others. You need to be committed to prayer and asking the Lord to give you direction and the right posture to address injustice in ways that edify rather than tear down.

But be prepared to walk down a road or two that is less traveled. It can be OK if you are alone. People may not be where you are. They may not be able to see what you see.

Is this a fun experience? Of course not! Not only are we made for others, but we derive confidence and strength from the support and camaraderie we receive from the people around us. When that's removed, we all struggle.

In the struggle, though, I want to encourage you to hang in there. Find ways to encourage yourself. Seek opportunities to find rest and recharge. Do what you need to do to continue to show up.

After all, so much of being just is simply showing up. And that can be hard to do when you are the only one and your intentions may not be quite right.

Marten, a White man, was new to his city and wanted to build trusting relationships with local African-American leaders. He was impacted by the injustices that were taking place related to race, and he knew he needed to understand those issues more deeply. He decided his first action step was to pursue more friends of color who could pour into him. So, when he was invited to an Interdenominational Ministerial Fellowship of primarily African-American pastors, he decided to attend.

As one of the few White people in the room, Marten felt a bit out of place. And in many ways, he was. Those in attendance wondered why he was there. They were used to having White people attend periodically, but that was because they had an agenda, and they assumed Marten was no different.

Marten believed his intentions were good, but he didn't realize the cost the ministers were bearing by accommodating what he hoped to gain from the time. They had work to do and were not that thrilled to "welcome" an outsider who wanted to benefit from knowing and interacting with them.

They graciously allowed Marten to attend their gatherings each week. As Marten kept coming, he began to see things in himself he never knew—how self-focused he had been, for instance, or how his presence initially had been a disruption rather than a blessing. Marten realized that the ways he was growing and becoming healthier were not a result of his perseverance, but the gracious love and selflessness he was receiving from this group of ministers.

Marten kept showing up, but he had to change in order for truly authentic relationships to form. And he did. Then they did. Over time, he naturally began attending their churches, prayer meetings, and service events in the community. He learned, behind the scenes, what life was like for them and the issues they faced.

Despite their hesitance at the beginning, many of the pastors pursued Marten as well. They joined him in "his world" and learned much from him.

It may not be pretty, but with the right posture and a willingness to stay the course despite your missteps, you might not feel so alone after all.

BE MISUNDERSTOOD

No matter how clear we are in the actions we take, we will routinely be misunderstood. People cannot see what we are seeing. If we are doing what's not popular, people will naturally question why we are doing what we are doing.

Again, we see this in the life of Jesus. He knew his mission clearly, and he repeated it often: He came to seek and save the lost, to preach the gospel, to heal, to redeem. At every turn, he was misunderstood. The Pharisees thought he was trying to overturn the whole religious system.

The disciples thought he was trying to organize a march on Rome. Just about the only ones in the Gospels who get Jesus's mission are the demons. (Not that they much liked it.)

What does this mean for us? How should we respond to the misunderstanding we're bound to face?

First, we need to be excellent communicators. This is Leadership 101, right? You see something others don't . . . yet. To get people on board, you need to paint the picture for them, cast the vision for what is possible. That's tough work.

Just leaders are able to articulate what they're seeing and know how to convey that to others. They use precise language instead of sweeping statements or overgeneralizations. We live in a world where things are so polarized that you have to be on one side or the other—one extreme or the other. And the communication we hear fits that. Just take twenty minutes and scroll through X. Actually, twenty seconds might do the trick. It won't take you long to see what sides people are on.

Emotionally charged communication may get a lot of response, but it doesn't chart a path forward in a fractured world. Just leaders recognize that for many issues, it's less either/or and more often both/and. It's more nuanced and complex, so they do everything they can to communicate that reality to others. They are thoughtful, measured, understanding of their audience, gracious, and engaging.

Second, we need to engage people in person, face-to-face, in voice-to-voice dialogue. I already mentioned this earlier, but social media is a terrible place to communicate and have "conversations" (or arguments) about issues of justice (or anything else for that matter). That place of interaction is wrought with misunderstanding. You can't determine tone, see facial expressions, or react in real time to what someone has said and pick up on the nuance. If you feel pressure to "be understood" on social media, I encourage you to simply let that go.

The same thing goes with sending emails or even writing blog posts. Written communication like this can work wonders (hello, I'm writing a book here). Keep doing it. Just know that if you are trying to be understood, the best way is always face-to-face, voice-to-voice.

Third, we need to be extremely patient and give people time to try to understand. They may never understand. That's tough to swallow, but just leaders accept that their role isn't to coerce others into change. Helping people understand issues of justice takes time, and many people do not have the context to be able to pick it up quickly. It takes tremendous patience and grace to walk with people through that.

Fourth, we need to pick our battles. Many times, it's not worth it to try to convince people (or certain people) to understand what we are doing. There's a place for engaging, winsome, inviting conversation. But there's also a time to realize you're beating your head against the wall. We need to understand what issues to address and what ones to let go of, which people we should continue to engage and which ones we should avoid.

FACE CRITICISM

Jesus was our model for the first two, and he's definitely our model here. Despite his huge popularity at the beginning of his ministry, by the end, every major power had turned against him. The crowds jeered at him. The religious leaders said he was blaspheming. The political leaders mocked his claims to be a king. From the world's perspective, they had only one word for Jesus—no.

We'll never experience that level of rejection and criticism. But it's encouraging to know that when we are criticized, we stand in good company.

On one of my visits to Ferguson, Missouri, I decided to go for a run. When I travel for work, I really enjoy running—not only for exercise but also to see and explore new cities. On the day I went for a run, there was snow on the ground that had covered the sidewalks. The only way to run safely was to run in the middle of the street.

I was in a residential neighborhood, so traffic was not a problem. It also was a Saturday morning, so people were just waking up to begin their day. Even though I was a stranger, I didn't think twice about running in a neighborhood I did not know. Not once did I wonder if people in the neighborhood would look out their window and wonder who this man running down the middle of the street was.

Then it hit me—my privilege.

As a White man, I did not consider at all what it would look like for me, a stranger, to run down the middle of the street. I never have been considered a threat, nor would someone think I had done something wrong and was running from something.

Just the day before, a few miles away from where I was running, I had gone to Canfield Drive, the street where Michael Brown was fatally shot by a police officer while walking down the middle of the street. The circumstances were entirely different, but it was not lost on me that I did not have to worry, as a White male, what it would look like for me to run down the middle of the street. If I were Black, it would not have been wise to go for a run, as a stranger, in the middle of a residential street in Ferguson.

That was a tangible moment for me when I truly recognized a measure of privilege because of my status as White. When I returned home from my trip, I wrote about it in a blog post and sent it to my network. I called it "My White Privilege."

I was shocked at the blowback. Sure, there were many positive reactions to what I wrote. But there was a lot of criticism. People pushed back on the idea of White privilege. They did not like the term and felt it discounted the hard work and obstacles many White people have overcome to achieve success. A few said Michael Brown deserved to be shot. After all, he had stolen something from the corner convenience store and did not respond appropriately to the police. They said I should be focused on other issues and not bring people into the messiness of social justice. They wondered why I would talk about something so controversial.

I was discouraged. I had hoped my experience would help people see and feel some of the pain of this community. Instead, I was being called to defend myself and told I was speaking out of turn. I felt dismissed.

Was I wrong to write the blog post?

I don't think so. I took a risk (a small one, at that, with very little cost), and risks come with potential downsides. In this case, it came with criticism.

None of us delights in criticism. But we should see, in criticism, an opportunity. I could have heard all of the critiques from my post and gone wrong in one of two ways—either dismissing everyone who wrote to me or caving and never speaking up again. Instead, I tried to enter into the mess, addressing people's concerns and starting honest conversations about the issues at play.

Often, our response to criticism matters more than what prompted the criticism in the first place! Not only does it help us build our justice muscles, but it allows us a chance to help others do the same.

TYLER'S RESPONSE

Let's revisit our friend Tyler. Tyler was able to identify a crew of two African American men who were willing to take on the job at the shopping center. He told the property manager they would be there that evening to clean the parking lot. When the crew arrived, they saw forty to sixty spaces with names honoring the recent victims of police shootings.

Two things surprised them. One was the material used; they expected paint, but the pictures were made using sidewalk chalk. The other surprise was the style of the writing: Each space featured one person's name, but it was situated with flowers at the top of the parking space. They were made to look like gravesites.

The team didn't know what to do. They hadn't realized just how extensive this was. And since it was chalk, not paint, they knew rain would easily wash the chalk away. It felt less like vandalism to them and more like a memorial. Given the racial tension taking place, they didn't want to be seen as the company washing away the memorial.

The crew manager reached out to the property manager: "We aren't in a position to complete the job tonight. But we don't want to simply leave you without options; we promise to work with you to come up with another solution."

The property manager wasn't having it. The next morning, she called, expressing her anger with the crew manager and with Tyler. She was getting tremendous pressure from the property owners, many of whom were demanding her to have it cleaned *immediately*. She was upset that Tyler's crew did not complete the job and threatened to not use Tyler's company in the future.

Tyler fully backed his crew and responded to the manager's concerns, taking responsibility for the decisions while sympathizing with her tough situation. He prides himself on having a company that does what it says it's going to do—finish the job—but the circumstances were just too unique for them to complete it that evening.

He offered a solution. It was more complicated than just cleaning the spaces, but he felt it was more just. He would 1) have a professional drone photographer take an overhead picture to capture the memorial, 2) provide signage that day letting customers know it was fine to park in the spaces as a way to honor those represented in the drawings, 3) create signage letting everyone know when the parking lot would be cleaned, and finally, 4) send a crew that evening to clean the parking spaces.

I'd like to say that the property manager loved his solution and accepted it. While she did appreciate his flexibility, she didn't go for the solution. She felt she had to have the lot cleaned immediately, so she found another company that was willing to do it that afternoon.

Tyler lost a job. He risked losing a customer. All because he was not willing to do what was popular—just complete the job. That would have been normal for him. But he could not do normal in this case. He had to be just, and being just took a risk.

A risk worth taking.

QUESTIONS TO CONSIDER

1. If you were Tyler, what would you have done?

2. What is normal that you should not consider normal anymore, because it's unjust?

3. Which of the challenges in this chapter is hardest for you—going alone, being misunderstood, or facing criticism?

4. What unpopular step do you need to take to confront an injustice?

CHAPTER 18

Action That's Disruptive

I walked into the Jobs for Life meeting and could tell something was up. Our staff was usually upbeat and energized by the work on their plates, but today was different. I could tell something was bothering them.

I asked a few probing questions, and we began to have one of those conversations where I knew I needed to pay careful attention.

They said we were doing an outstanding job preparing people for work, but our students were still not getting livable wage jobs. We weren't certain our students were going to companies with leaders who knew how to help them thrive at work. Some of their new employers were abrasive, even toxic. Plus, in some cities where JfL operates, there just weren't any jobs.

In addition, many of our students needed more than the training we were providing for them. They needed to be challenged to dream and think far beyond just being a good employee. They needed to see themselves as owners, people with the ability and capacity to run businesses. They needed to see themselves represented in positions of power and leadership so they would believe the dream, "That might be me one day."

My team reminded me that preparing people for work was a worthy goal. But we couldn't pretend it was fixing everything. The ultimate goal was to help them not only find work, but find meaningful, edifying work that helped them excel and take care of themselves and their families. One team member put it plainly: "If we don't keep our eye on people *thriving* at work, we simply haven't accomplished our mission."

I knew they were right. For the longest time, I was laser-focused on helping the organizations we served at JfL have the tools and training to prepare men and women for work. I thought that if we could just teach individuals God's design for work and connect students to a community of people who could help them find good jobs, everything would take care of itself. After all, that was what we could control. Why stress about the rest?

I had failed to understand the breadth and depth of the system of work in our country. That system played a huge role in the outcomes of our students. And if we were to accomplish our mission, the flaws in that system had to be addressed—even disrupted.

If we didn't do something to help employers see their role—to provide livable wage jobs, to create environments for people to thrive, to figure out how have patience with people who needed time to overcome physical and emotional barriers, to inspire investment and training for men and women to start businesses—then the work we were doing to prepare people for work would continually encounter dead ends.

In essence, we needed to disrupt a broken system.

MORE THAN JUST A FISH

Just leaders take action that's disruptive.

Like Paul and Silas in Philippi, our efforts to bring healing and blessing might not immediately be welcome. "They are disturbing the city," was the reply those men got—mostly since they had healed and liberated a slave girl, and her owners didn't like losing their "property" (see Acts 16:19–20). In a fractured community, healing and just action will feel disruptive, even transgressive. But the alternative is leaving our community the way it is. And if we're people of justice, we'll simply care too much to leave everything the way we found it.

In first-century Philippi, disruptive action looked like a miraculous healing of a slave girl. What does disruptive action look like in twenty-first-century United States?

It begins by recognizing that we cannot simply address individual behavior; we must be able to see and have the courage to disrupt broken systems.

We've already talked about the idea of a "system" in Quality 2 on cultural competency. Remember the older fish asking the two younger fish how the water was? If you recall, one of the younger fish said, "What the hell is water?"

Fish don't know they're in water, just like we might not recognize we are part of a culture.

The same analogy can be used when thinking about systems. We typically don't think about the systems around us. They're just the water we swim in, the air we breathe, and the assumptions that seem obvious and universal.

The Racial Equity Institute (REI), based in Greensboro, North Carolina, uses the same analogy in its Groundwater Project. But in this one, the fish aren't talking. They're dying:

If you have a lake in front of your house and one fish is floating belly-up dead, it makes sense to analyze the fish. What is wrong with it? Imagine the fish is one student failing in the education system. We'd ask: did it study hard enough? Is it getting the support it needs at home? But if you come out to that same lake and half the fish are floating belly-up dead, what should you do? This time you've got to analyze the lake. Imagine the lake is the education system and half the students are failing. This time we'd ask: might the system itself be causing such consistent, unacceptable outcomes for students? If so, how? Now . . . picture five lakes around your house, and in each and every lake half the fish are floating belly-up dead! What is it time to do? We say it's time to analyze the groundwater.[67]

What my JfL team told me that day was that, in essence, we were rehabilitating a lot of individual fish—but we just kept sending them back into the same toxic pond.

It's natural—and to some extent, helpful—to start with the individual. But if our focus stays there indefinitely, we're going to find ourselves "fixing" the same problem over and over again. Only the problem doesn't get fixed. We keep addressing fish problems, and the fish keep dying.

We need to bring the groundwater into the lab.

WHAT EXACTLY IS A SYSTEM?

REI helps people understand how a number of interlocking systems contribute to racial inequity in the United States. REI tries to lift our gaze higher than individual negative outcomes for communities of color, investigating the "groundwater" that makes those outcomes more probable.

But racism isn't the only system-level problem. Let's back up and define what we mean by systems.

A system is, in its simplest form, any set of parts that together make a coherent whole. A physical system is the easiest to imagine: My Honda Pilot is a system, composed of a couple tons of metal and computer chips. Each element is necessary for the entire system to function. But most elements do their thing without me thinking about them. (I'm still not sure which one is the carburetor.)

Intangible systems are more difficult to grasp, but they are every bit as real as my Pilot. Rather than being composed of physical objects, intangible systems are composed of norms, expectations, and practices. Together, they give the impression that *this is the way things are done*. The system can even run by itself, without much planning or initiative by a person or group.

Think of an intangible system like a waterfall. The waterfall is the result of a complex number of factors. In that way, it has certain "rules" it follows. But the waterfall seems to just, well . . . happen.

Or imagine yourself at a basketball game. The environment of the game is a system that nudges you toward certain behaviors (and away from others). You will wear certain colors. You will sit and stand in a rhythmic pattern. You will shout. You might even find yourself singing with twenty thousand strangers. None of this behavior is what you *normally* do. But it's what the system of a basketball game requires. As you enter the system—assuming you know how basketball games work—you enter the world that system creates.

When we take this idea and apply it to race, it becomes easy to understand why so many people advocate for *very big* changes—system-wide changes—to our society. For instance, Martin Luther King Jr. put it this way, "White Americans must recognize that justice for Black people cannot be achieved without radical changes in the structure of our society."[68]

In other words, it's not enough merely to love people who are different from us. We need to be willing to disrupt broken systems of injustice.

But don't get stuck on the racial application. Remember, systems don't only affect racial disparities. They affect just about every inequity in our society. Here are a few:

The Employment System: We like to think of the United States as a meritocracy, where the best opportunities go to the best-qualified individuals. But it takes very little time in the business world to realize that not every applicant enters the process on an equal footing. Great applicants are often overlooked. Others never even apply. And for those who do manage to get work, far too many find they aren't able to support themselves, even with a full-time salary.

The Education System: In the educational world, resources are king. So it shouldn't surprise us that schools in low-income areas find themselves under-resourced—and, as a result, in continual decay. Individual students may, nearly miraculously, make their way out. But the "groundwater" in many schools is incredibly harmful.

The Criminal Justice System: Sometimes, this comes as a result of policy; other times, it comes as a result of enforcement. Either way, certain groups of people tend to be incarcerated more often and more harshly than others, even for the same crimes. Our legal system, which should allow equal access to justice, still strongly favors those who have financial wealth.

The Housing System: Ordinances sometimes restrict affordable housing development, pushing developers to focus on the projects that actually make them money—those for middle- and upper-class neighborhoods.

Much more could be said about each of these systems. They are, by their nature, incredibly complex. My point here isn't to offer the easy fix for each system, but to paint a picture of the types of systems that just leaders need to be aware of.

SYSTEMIC OR SYSTEMATIC?

When referring to systems, people often use the words systemic and systematic. They use them interchangeably, but they have different meanings.

Systematic refers to something done according to process or plan. A good way to remember what systematic means is that it rhymes with *automatic*. Something that is performed systematically may appear to be almost automatic in its smoothness. When Starbucks transforms your order into reality—and within ninety seconds you're holding a tall half-caff dark chocolate mocha latte (or whatever your favorite drink is)—they're operating in a wonderfully *systematic* way.

Systemic refers to something that *affects* an entire system—as in "system-wide." Systemic issues aren't usually as overt and intentional, but they can be just as pervasive and powerful.[69] For instance, when you get sick, your body has a *systemic* problem. Everything is affected.

Or, when an organization suffers from low morale, it has a *systemic* problem. Everyone is affected. It's not likely that there's a rule on the HR books that is forcing everyone to hate their work or their supervisor. Something more intangible is going on. But the intangibility doesn't lessen the force one iota.

Systematic and *systemic* have often been used to describe racism in our country. To understand the difference, here are a couple of examples:

Systematic racism is a set of practices that discriminate on the basis of race. These are overt. Think "Whites only" water fountains or segregated restaurants during Jim Crow or people of color having to sit in the back of the bus. These are clearly racist policies and practices. They are automatic, intentional, part of the plan.

Systemic racism describes a system that has racism within it, *whether or not it's part of the "plan."* This is a bit trickier to detect. It's not as overt, and because of that, it can have a deeper impact.

The GI Bill is a good example of systemic racism. It was not set up legally to be a policy that discriminated based on race. On the books, it was available to everyone. But how it was applied revealed systemic racism. Bankers, nearly all White, applied the loans to people they felt were worthy of the risk, and they chose White people instead of Black or Brown people. Because racism was inherent in the people applying the policy, they demonstrated systemic racism.

Why does this seemingly hairsplitting distinction matter?

Remember, to be just leaders, even world-class leaders, we need to be aware of these slight differences so we can take action in the correct way. If we don't rightly understand the problem we're facing, we'll find ourselves consistently applying the wrong solution. We'll keep "fixing" dying fish.

Systems are *both* systematic (more overt, part of the plan) and systemic (more covert, below the surface). Just leaders see both. Just leaders will learn to disrupt both.

"I DON'T BUY THE IDEA OF SYSTEMIC ANYTHING"

Before we talk about how to disrupt systems for justice, I want to acknowledge that many people really struggle with the concept of systems. Maybe that's you. You don't buy the idea of systematic or systemic *anything*. Perhaps you feel that most injustice is a result of individual decisions and behaviors and the consequences that come from those behaviors.

In my experience, this pushback arises from two big ideas:

1. If we focus on the systemic, we give excuses for people's behavior. This gives everyone a get-out-of-jail-free card, which actually hurts them more than it helps them.
2. If we focus on the systemic, we undermine the good that was accomplished. Not everything in our society or in our history is categorically bad, and talking about "broken systems" leads us to bash history, wipe away history, or join the toxic "cancel culture" that's always looking to cancel the latest offender.

On the one hand, I agree with that. We *can* get too caught up in the past and blame all of our problems on what was handed down to us. And we *can* be way too negative and not recognize and celebrate the positive. The United States in 2023 is not the same as it was in 1923 (or, for that matter, 1823), and we need to be honest about that.

Of course, injustice is a result of individuals and their actions. Focusing on systems as a key contributor to problems should never overlook individual injustice. We have so many examples of unjust leaders who must be stopped, whether they are public figures or people we encounter every day. Individual justice still matters.

Nor should we discourage people from taking responsibility for their lives and their futures. We help people best by equipping them to face the challenges ahead, not by eliminating every challenge for them.

But if injustice can be done by individuals, it can also make its way into systems created and run by individuals. Systemic injustice doesn't mean that all inequity is the result of systems. It simply means that systems are always a relevant factor. Unjust decisions made by individuals over time become baked into our systems, such that, in and of themselves, they are unjust. *Both* individuals *and* systems can be agents of injustice.

The good news is that *both* individuals *and* systems can be agents of justice, too. Which is precisely why your disruptive action matters.

SIX WAYS JUST LEADERS CAN DISRUPT BROKEN SYSTEMS

So, what exactly is required to disrupt an unjust system? If injustice is "baked into" a system, is our only option to throw away the cake and start over? Should we all become revolutionaries?

I don't think so. I believe that just leaders can disrupt many broken systems without tearing them down completely. It will take incredible effort and creativity, but it's possible.

Dr. King provides a bit of a roadmap here for us. During Illinois Wesleyan's Convocation in 1966, he said:

And it may well be that we will have to repent in this generation, not merely for the vitriolic words and the violent actions of the bad people who would bomb a church in Birmingham, Alabama but for the appalling silence and indifference of the good people who sit around and say wait on time. Somewhere we must come to see that human progress never rolls in on the wheels of inevitability. It comes through the tireless efforts and the persistent work of dedicated individuals who are willing to be co-workers with God. And without this hard work, time itself becomes an ally of the primitive forces of social stagnation. And so it is necessary to help time and to realize that the time is always right to do right.[70]

What does it look like to "do right" in the midst of broken systems? What does disruptive action look like? I believe there are six features to disruptive action, several of which arise directly from Dr. King's Illinois Wesleyan speech—repentance, savvy, trust, urgency, sacrifice, and longsuffering.

To show how these six features operate, I want to end by briefly imagining a hypothetical leadership situation. Let's say that you manage a temp agency. The goal of the organization is good—helping connect qualified candidates to employers in need of new employees. But you've come to realize that you might only be addressing "fish problems," and you'd like to think about the groundwater as well.

1. Repentance. The first step is probably the hardest: Repent for the ways that you have not paid attention to broader employment issues before—or even for ways you have contributed to a broken system.

To do this faithfully, you'll have to really spend time learning about your organization's history and its impact in the community. Perhaps, as you learn more, you'll realize that you have been screening out applicants without college education, even though none of your placement options require a degree. Perhaps you'll learn that your applicants are entering workplaces that treat them poorly or pay them less than contracted amounts.

Whatever you find, be open to learning about the problems around you, even if you can't fix them.

2. Savvy. Once you start to see some of the systemic problems in and around your organization, you'll need knowledge and understanding—not only to correctly *diagnose* the problem (hard enough), but also to know how to address it. Understand the complexity of the problem in front of you, know where to start, and recognize that you can't solve the whole problem, but you can tackle part of it.

For instance, if you know your applicants are being placed in bad work environments, you have your work cut out for you. Your role isn't to create new jobs. Your role is not to raise pay. Your role is to try to ensure that your organization is not funneling applicants into bad work environments.

How will you address this issue? That's where your savvy comes in. It might be something you can resolve directly with the companies who are hiring. It might be something you address through the contracts you write up. It might be some other solution. Don't settle, just because it's been this way for a while.

3. Trust. Build trust, both with people in power and those who have been hurt by the system. All the savvy in the world won't help if no one believes that you're there to help. So make the investment. Trust takes a lot of time. It's inefficient. It's messy. But there's no other way.

In our hypothetical example, the needle you'll have to thread is building trust both with your incoming applicants (who are wary of being placed in toxic environments) and with your existing companies (who are reluctant to have you tell them how to operate). You don't have to think both groups are in the right. But you do have to spend the time putting yourself in the shoes of both.

4. Urgency. Unless something has risen to the level of a crisis, it's easy to postpone dealing with messy systemic issues. Something more pressing is always there to claim our attention. But if we want to be just leaders, we can't just wait for the "right" time. As Dr. King said, the time is always right to do right.

Imagine that the issue you've identified isn't something that only affects your organization. Imagine that it impacts you—that you were the temp employee walking unknowingly into a terrible placement. Wouldn't you want someone to address that issue *sooner* rather than *later*?

5. Sacrifice. As much as we would like it to be otherwise, pursuing justice is often going to cost us—time, money, reputation, friendships, comfort, control. And part of our fear in acting disruptively is that *we don't know what we will have to sacrifice!*

At your temp agency, as with any organization, the inertia will lean toward the status quo. And the moment you decide to address this unjust systemic issue, you'll begin to learn why it has lingered for so long. A high-status co-worker pulls you aside to tell you to stop meddling. A few companies with long-standing partnerships cancel their contracts. You run the numbers on the changes you've imagined, and you realize it will increase operating costs by 8 percent.

When the sacrifice becomes tangible, you know you're headed in the right direction. But it takes courage to keep moving.

6. Longsuffering. For disruptive change to make any positive difference, it has to be marked by patience, perseverance, faithfulness, and follow-through. The world has seen enough passionate people catch fire and burn out. What it needs more of are people who will continue to repent, act, and sacrifice even as the waters get choppier. Just leaders are in it for the long haul.

To which you might ask, *How can I stick it out for the long haul?* Great question. Turn the page and find out.

QUESTIONS TO CONSIDER

1. How do you react to the reality of broken systems? Do you acknowledge they are real? Ignore them? Feel paralyzed by them?
2. What systems are you a part of or do you work with?
3. What would make those systems more just?
4. Which steps to address broken systems do you resonate with? Which ones make you pause? (Repentance, Savvy, Trust, Urgency, Sacrifice, Longsuffering)

CHAPTER 19

Action That's Slow

Well, you've gotten to the end of the book. We've covered a lot of ground. I've given you much to consider about becoming a just leader. Maybe you're feeling overwhelmed. Maybe you're feeling inspired. Either way, now is the time for me to *pump you up and send you out*, right? To give you that iconic speech that makes you charge out of the locker room, ready to take on whatever opponent you have to face. To be the leader you have always wanted to be. To change your community—or even change the world.

So, are you ready for your inspiration? Ready to be pumped up? Here goes:

Slow down.

Wait, what? Did you say slow? That's the inspiration? The speech to get me fired up? What a downer! You have to be kidding me right? *Slow down?*

Sorry for the disappointment. I wish I could make it up to you. But it's true: Just leaders take action that's *slow*.

Now, before you decide to go find another, more inspiring locker-room speech, hear me out. You might be surprised, even inspired, by what this means for you.

Remember the *urgency* we talked about in the last chapter? *Slow* doesn't mean *wait*. It certainly doesn't mean *stop*. But some of the best changes in life take time. They can't be rushed. And justice is like that. There is no microwave for justice. Only slow cookers.

So, by all means, *keep moving*. Keep learning. Keep acting. But realize that the most profound impact of your action is likely to be slow. Some just leaders see dramatic changes in short periods of time. Most don't. But your impact is still real. It simply can't be measured in hours or days. It's a matter of weeks, months, years.

Even generations.

So let me inspire you. Your actions today, the results of which *you may never see*, are for your children, your children's children, or your children's children's children's children. You must act today with a sense of urgency so future generations can experience what you hope to change.

It reminds me of Moses, who led the people of God out of slavery in Egypt. Moses saw some incredible things. He was there for the ten plagues, miraculous signs of God's liberating power. He saw an ocean split in two. He saw God's presence in the pillar of fire and the pillar of cloud. He spoke with God *directly* on multiple occasions. You'd be hard-pressed to think of an Old Testament figure who saw more dramatic and immediate change than Moses.

Yet, everything in Moses's life was aimed at one goal—to get God's people to the Promised Land. Here's the irony: Moses himself never got to go in. For forty years after they left Egypt, Moses led God's people in the wilderness. When the moment came to enter the Promised Land, God told Moses that he wouldn't be going. His time had come to be with God himself.

Just think of it: Moses, on top of a mountain, watching a nation of millions marching forward to the land God had promised them—a land he would never enjoy.

I've often heard Moses's story told with a note of bitterness, as if Moses must have been upset that he wouldn't enjoy the Promised Land. I don't read it that way. I imagine Moses watching God's people and thinking, "I got to be a part of that. For centuries to come, people I don't even know will enjoy this land . . . all because I was faithful to the moment God gave me."

I don't know about you, but I would love to have an impact like that. In our quick fix world, generational impact like that is unheard of. If you're a leader who's wired to fix things, that can be a bit disconcerting. Fixing things is about getting results now, measuring outcomes, solving problems. But fixing things isn't the same as flourishing. If you want to thrive, if you want to pursue justice, then your fix-it mindset is not your friend.

To be the leader you are designed and called to be, you must have a long-term vision—one that spans the test of time, does not waver in the face of adversity, and is not all about (get ready for it) you.

So, let me give you a pep talk. Being about generational impact requires it.

This is not for the faint of heart. Remember, we truly are trying to build world-class leadership by helping leaders understand what it means to be just. That takes more than wishful thinking. It takes grit. But that's not new for you, is it? You are a professional, you operate with different standards, and you have the will and the stamina most people do not have. If you're faithful to apply what you've learned in this book, you now have a perspective that goes beyond what everyone else sees. You can navigate cultural competency that's nuanced and filled with land mines. You understand power and what it takes to give power away.

You're ready to transform your community from a fractured one into a flourishing one.

And you're smart enough to know that things won't change overnight. The road ahead is going to be a long one. So you're ready to pack your bags for the journey.

The question is: *What should you pack in your bag?* What do you need to keep moving, slowly but surely? Allow me to offer you four parting gifts for the road ahead.

GIFT #1: FAITH

The writer of Hebrews put it well: "Now faith is the assurance of things hoped for, the conviction of things not seen" (Hebrews 11:1). Faith propelled the great saints of the Bible, from Abraham to Moses to Rahab to David. It gave them courage to follow God when everyone else thought they were crazy. It gave them front-row seats to miracles and military victories and healings. It gave them the strength to continue trusting in God even when their lives were marked by suffering and loss.

Hebrews 11 ends this way: "And all these, though commended through their faith, did not receive what was promised, since God had provided something better for us, that apart from us they should not be made perfect" (Hebrews 11:39–40). We may not consider our faith like that of Moses or Abraham. But their faith is stitched together with ours. And they are cheering us on, urging us to exercise the same faith in our day.

These saints of old say to us, "Have faith in God." This is fundamental. To keep walking the road of justice, we need faith in God, believing that he is with us, that he will never leave us nor forsake us. He is guiding us every step of the way.

They say to us, "Have faith in others." You may feel alone, but you also will need to trust and have faith in others. Bring others along with you. Encourage them, rely on them, even if they disappoint or don't follow through.

They say to us, "Have faith in yourself." Believe you have done the work to move forward; you have done your homework; you have seen what you need to see; you have understood the problem; you know the steps to take. Have you achieved perfection? Hardly. But God can use your imperfect faithfulness to make your community a more just place—less fractured, more flourishing.

You have a plan, but that plan may be more gray than black-and-white. That's OK. You will need to keep walking, often blindly entering into certain situations not knowing exactly what's ahead. Don't back down. You've been prepared for this.

GIFT #2: A DIFFERENT MEASURING STICK

If you've ever traveled outside the United States, you know the confusion of trying to gauge distances in kilometers. I know the math involved isn't terribly complicated, but it's always thrown me. Especially if I'm driving around, when I quickly glance at the speed limit sign and it says 80 kph, I legitimately don't know what to do. *Wait, kilometers are smaller . . . does that mean the speed is slower or faster? Should I be going 45 mph or 120 mph? 120 seems way too fast, but . . .* And by this time, I'm already half a mile (or 805 meters) down the road.

Pursuing justice is a bit like that. The measuring tools you had before aren't always the ones you'll need in the future. You need to adjust to a new system to know if you're on the right track or not.

We've talked about what success looks like and how different it is when pursuing justice. Success is broad and can be difficult to gauge. How can it be measured accurately? What should we even be measuring? And how much of that is within our control?

Certainly, there *are* quantifiable outcomes we can measure. Here are just a handful:

- Are people building wealth?
- Do underrepresented voices have a seat at the table?
- Are policies equitable?
- Are resources distributed fairly?
- Are people being held accountable for unjust actions?
- Are underserved people groups having more positive outcomes— higher graduation rates, employment, ownership, influence?
- Are incarceration rates going down?
- Is home ownership increasing across all people groups?
- Is the poverty rate decreasing?

Quantifiable outcomes are helpful. But they are not the only ones to gauge whether we are cultivating and multiplying justice. Other outcomes, while much more subjective, are just as important.

Remember what we talked about in Chapter 4—the characteristics of a rejoicing city? A city of justice is marked by:

- Beauty
- Unity
- Security
- Lack of violence
- Wholeness
- Hope
- Comfort
- Economic flourishing
- Sustainability
- Peace with God

How do you measure beauty, unity, wholeness, and hope? How can you tell when a community's fractures are beginning to heal? In a sense, we know it when we see it. But it's difficult to describe with numbers.

A thriving and just community is felt as much as it is measured. It comes through in emotions, attitudes, even beliefs. It comes from a sense of belonging to one another and having a common mission. Much of this is below the surface, not above it, but when you experience it, you don't forget it.

These are qualities that take time to cultivate. But they are worth the investment.

GIFT #3: CHILDREN

If you are a parent, you will need to include your children. It's surprising to me how often leaders overlook this ever-present application. For some reason, we think that justice happens "out there" in the world, not "in here" in our homes. We forget that what we cultivate in our children doesn't stay "in here" forever.

Pour into your children. Help them see what you see. As a parent, I feel like I fail more than I succeed with my kids. I feel I haven't taught them as much as I want or given them as many experiences as I had hoped.

Every child is different, but as our kids have grown, I have learned they are resilient, able to handle more than I expect, and are learning far more than I think, even from me. It's often the little things, too. It's the things I overlook that impact them the most. They are watching when I least expect it.

And ultimately, they are the means through which many of our efforts toward justice will be realized. I may not see the results of my actions, but they will. It's OK for them to see and experience injustices, to face hardship, to deal with pain.

That's a tough lesson for any parent. I want to protect my kids from pain, adversity, and discomfort. I don't want them to experience failure or injustice. Instead, I want them to have a nice, sweet, comfortable life.

But as hard as it is, that's not what they really need. The road to thriving isn't paved with comfort. It's paved with honest attempts to grapple with justice.

My kids don't need to live in a bubble. Instead, they need to see how to face and overcome failure, how to interact with injustice around them, and how to develop a vision for the ways they can be just. They need to see the fractures in their community so they can dream about the ways God might use them to heal those fractures.

If we can instill even a bit of that, our kids will be more ready than we think.

During the early stages of the COVID-19 pandemic, when everyone was quarantining and families were at home, our family of six was together in a way we did not expect. Our kids were college age, so we suddenly had time with them that we would never have again.

Despite the devastating effects of the pandemic, we were blessed to be together.

I am keenly aware that not every family had such a blessed experience. Along with pervasive sickness and death, the pandemic was a time of deep political and racial unrest in our country. Every day, it seemed, there was more bad news. The fractures were only growing.

One night, I turned to my kids and said, "I wish you guys did not have to grow up with all of this—the pandemic, the political unrest, the riots, the divisions, the pain . . . the death. I hurt for your generation."

And one of our children responded by saying, "We've got this, Dad. We're made for this."

His words totally turned my perspective upside down. He's right. Things aren't hopeless, and I do not have to be the one to carry the torch. My children can. So can their children. And so can *their* children. This game is not over. We may feel like we're in the fourth quarter and down by twenty points, but there is a lot more game to be played. And there are young, talented players getting ready to get in the game. Let's give them the ball . . . and watch them work.

GIFT #4: OBSCURITY

Obscurity doesn't sound like a gift. Nobody wants to work on the margins, ignored in this life and forgotten when they're gone. I want to assure you that obscurity is precious. It's not a problem to overcome; it's food for the journey.

We all want to be people who are remembered, who leave a legacy, who make something of ourselves, to have our name on a building, to be written about in history books.

But you know what? It's OK to be forgotten. In fact, it's *more* than OK.

You don't have to worry about leaving a legacy. You don't need your name on a building. You can have tremendous impact *and never be recognized for it*. For the just leader, what matters isn't whether other people notice. What matters is whether we're cultivating justice in the world around us.

There are two reasons just leaders embrace obscurity. The first is that being just is not about you; it's about others.

But there is a deeper reason: *More often than not, the most healing and transformative work you do will be unseen*. People won't even know it was you.

Even people outside of a biblical faith understand this. Ancient Chinese philosopher Lao Tzu said, "A leader is best when people barely know he exists. When his work is done, his aim fulfilled, they will say: *we did it ourselves.*"

Other people will end up taking the credit for work you did. They will have no idea you were behind the scenes, making things happen, pulling people together, sacrificing your time, quietly praying, feeling the burden, making the decision, giving the money. You were the one breaking the waves so others could operate in clear, calm waters. And no one will know that's what you were even doing.

They just thought the waters were calm and went off to celebrate while you were overlooked, forgotten.

When that happens, don't be bitter. Don't be worried. Be encouraged. You're on the right path. You've traded fractured for flourishing—not just for you, but for everyone around you.

So join Moses on the mountaintop. Embrace the obscurity. Take a step back and enjoy the view. Because for centuries to come, people you don't even know will taste the fruit of your flourishing . . . all because you were faithful to follow the God of justice.

QUESTIONS TO CONSIDER

1. Which notion of becoming a just leader challenges you more— slowing down or embracing obscurity? Why?
2. If being a just leader is a journey that spans across generations, how does that change how you view yourself?
3. Where are you sensing God leading you in this journey? What does it look like to take a step forward today?

The Just Leader

For the leaders we coach at 11 Ten Leadership, we use two assessments to gauge the level at which they are thriving and being just—since, as we've seen throughout this book, those two pathways are actually one.

The first is a THRIVE Assessment, which measures how well leaders are thriving and how well those they lead are thriving. Along with an overall score, it captures the leader's and their team's effectiveness in each of the areas I described in Chapter 14: Trust, Health, Relationships, Impact, Value, and Engagement (THRIVE).

If you'd like more information on the THRIVE Assessment, contact us at info@11tenleadership.com.

The second is a Just Leadership Assessment. I have provided a sample of the Just Leadership Assessment here. This captures many of the ideas described in the book, providing a benchmark to help you know where you are doing well and where you could use more work.

Whether you jumped here before you started the book or you've just finished it, this assessment can be a baseline for you and help you think through your own next steps.

We use a comprehensive rating and scoring system for leaders and their teams, but for now, simply answer "yes" or "no" to each statement below.

And remember, this won't be helpful to you if you try to give the "right" answer to each question. Be honest.

JUST LEADER ASSESSMENT

1. I know what my strengths are as a leader.
2. I know the areas in which I need to grow as a leader.
3. I am aware of the implicit biases I have of others.
4. I know the dreams of the people I lead.
5. I know the history of the community in which I live and work.
6. I know the issues in my city that keep people from thriving.
7. I have a number of close relationships with people of a different ethnicity than me ("close" meaning they consider you a trusted friend).
8. I have a number of close relationships with people in material need ("close" meaning they consider you a trusted friend).
9. I have a number of close relationships with people of a different sexual orientation than me ("close" meaning they consider you a trusted friend).
10. I am being led or mentored by leaders of a different ethnicity than me.
11. I spend time in contexts where I am the minority or "the other."
12. I spend time in the areas of my community where people in material need live.
13. At our company/organization, we are just as concerned about the impact we are having as we are about profit.
14. I sacrificially give my money away.
15. I try to find ways to provide opportunities to people who have historically not had access to power or resources.
16. I look for ways to disadvantage myself for the advantage of others.
17. At our company/organization, we measure the extent to which our people are thriving.
18. At our company/organization, we measure the extent to which our work helps our community thrive.
19. I am OK to risk my network to address something that is unjust.

20. I feel prepared to speak up when something is unjust, even though most others are afraid of saying the wrong thing.
21. We have a culture at our company/organization that identifies and confronts actions that treat people unfairly.
22. Our company/organization is willing to confront practices within our industry that treat people unfairly.
23. I have a sense of urgency to do something when I see injustice.
24. I am someone who is willing to stick it out over the long haul, even when progress is small or takes time.

The average leader responds "yes" to twelve to fifteen of the statements above and "no" to the rest. How do you compare?

Remember, being just is a journey, not a destination, and we'd be happy to help you along the way.

For additional insight and other resources, check out our website at 11tenleadership.com.

ACKNOWLEDGMENTS

Writing my first book is certainly a milestone, and I could not have done it without the support, affirmation, and work of so many people.

First, to Alice, my wife, who said I could actually do this. I learned the first step to writing a book is simply believing I can do it and trusting I have something worth sharing. Alice instilled that in me from the very beginning and helped me believe it even when I didn't. She is and always has been my biggest fan. I love you, Alice, with all my heart.

And to our children, Ben, Scott, Meg, and Claire, who have walked this journey with us and trusted us as their parents. They have lived out so many of the ideas conveyed in this book, which has been a blessing for Alice and me to watch and experience. They are a complete joy to us.

There would be no book without Chris Pappalardo, my editor from day one, who made the words on the page come alive in ways I could not do. His wisdom—and it seemed to me, *magic*—inspired and gave me the energy to push forward. He has the ability to help me weave words through the eye of a needle, capturing the right posture and feel for what I wanted to communicate, particularly with some delicate topics. (And there's no shortage of delicate topics in here!) No way could I have done this without him.

The same goes for Rob Shields, my colleague at 11 Ten Leadership. Rob did much of the leg work behind the scenes, not only reviewing and strengthening the content of the book but also finding and engaging key people who have been a part of this project. Along with Mary Ellen Bradford's support early on, he turned this from "my" project to "our" project, which is an incredible feeling to have. Both his and Mary Ellen's willingness to give of themselves for this book has provided me strength and support I didn't even realize I needed.

Special thanks to all those who read and reviewed early drafts of the book—Craig Stephenson, Daniel Alexander, LaToya King, Paul Green, Ken Jenkins, Geoff Bradford, Erik Hanvey, Micah Sedillos, Joy Currey, Jerome Gay, DJ Hill, Donna Harris, Phillip Walker, Shay Bassett, Rod Webb, Dax Palmer, Jon Mills, Ryan Ray, Scott Steele, my son Scott, and my brother, Anderson. They affirmed, pushed back, questioned, refined, and made the whole process better. If anything is still lacking, that's on me.

Thank you to all those who provided an endorsement for the book. They are not only experts in their respective fields but also great friends who have encouraged me in so many ways . . . both seen and unseen.

Thanks to all of the leaders at the companies and organizations with whom we have the privilege to work at 11 Ten Leadership. I'm grateful for trusting and allowing us to learn as they invest in their employees to help everyone win.

Thanks to all of the leaders who have been a part of Just Leadership groups, faithfully committed to engaging one another and growing in what it means to be the *tsaddiqim*. They have all taken a step of faith to be a part of this effort and inspired me for what is possible, as we steward all God has given us for his peace and justice.

To my friends and colleagues during my time at Jobs for Life—LaToya King, Shay Bassett, Daniel Alexander, Paul Green, Ken Jenkins, Beverly Jenkins, Ryan Ray, DJ Hill, Scott Steele, Stephanie Tarant, James White, Cynthia White, Bo Batchelder, Erik Hanvey, Byron McMillan, Alex Ford, Spencer Hathcock, Jessie Hathcock, Laurel Freeman, Marten Fadelle, Danny Rohrdanz, Keynon Akers, Miea Walker, Tracy Clark, Hanna Compton, Wendy Weber, Katie Straight, Paula Bryan, Skip Long, James Roberson, Beth Walkup, Rick Flammer, Suzanne Flammer, Reverend Frank Alexander, Reverend Stephen Tucker, Pastor Donald McCoy, Pat Mangum, and countless more, including leaders in cities across the country. They have taken on the JfL mission and pursued men and women in their communities with the dignity of work and the hope of Jesus. They all have shown me how big God really is.

Thanks to the life and example of Chris Mangum, co-founder of Jobs for Life. Much of what I have written is based on what I saw from Chris, whose life was the embodiment of the *tsaddiqim*. His words and actions are all over the pages of this book.

Thanks to my lifelong best friends—Erik, Scott, Joel, Randy, and Kevin. Our monthly calls serve to cover and strengthen me. These men are all a breath of fresh air (and sometimes even the oxygen I need) to be what God has designed me to be as a husband, father, and leader.

Thanks to Geoff Bradford, my pastor and friend, especially for our weekly walks. I can't put a price tag on the way his faithful pursuit of me has encouraged and galvanized me to follow Jesus.

Thanks to everyone at the Denver Institute for Faith & Work who have come alongside me and my team to promote the principles of *The Just Leader*.

Thanks to Claudia Volkman for copyediting and typesetting (whew!), Chelsea Malinaric for graphic design, and Dave Sheets for distribution. Without their work, I never would have gotten the book over the finish line.

And finally, to Mom, Dad, Susan, and Anderson: You have loved and shaped me from the beginning. Really, you are the wind behind my sails. I am forever grateful for the gift you are to me.

NOTES

1 http://www.maxshores.com/kudzu/;
http://www.ncsu.edu/goingnative/howto/mapping/invexse/kudzu.html.

2 https://reelrundown.com/misc/Catch-Me-If-You-Can-is-a-Movie-based-on-the-Real-Life-Story-of-Frank-Abagnale.

3 Herman Bavinck, John Bolt, and John Vriend, *Reformed Dogmatics: God and Creation*, vol. 2 (Grand Rapids: Baker Academic, 2004), 222.

4 Tim Keller, *Generous Justice: How God's Grace Makes Us Just* (London: Penguin, 2012), 4–5.

5 Brian Fikkert and Steve Corbett, *When Helping Hurts: How to Alleviate Poverty without Hurting the Poor . . . and Yourself* (Chicago: Moody Publishers, 2014), need to find page number.

6 Jemar Tisby, "Battle Lines Form over Social Justice: Is It Gospel or Heresy?, Religious News Service, September 6, 2018, https://religionnews.com/2018/09/06/battle-lines-form-over-social-justice-is-it-gospel-or-heresy/.

7 Tim Keller, "A Biblical Critique of Secular Justice and Critical Theory," September 2020, *Gospel in Life*, https://quarterly.gospelinlife.com/a-biblical-critique-of-secular-justice-and-critical-theory/.

8 Ibid.

9 Technically, the Jewish pattern of Sabbath was at the end of the week. The Christian reboot of Sabbath, though, moved it to the first day. But that's not to say that beginning with rest was a novelty in the first century. The Jewish understanding of the day began with rest. For the Jews, the day was "evening-morning," unlike our Western understanding of morning kicking off the day. In the Jewish rhythm, you began the day by resting and then awoke to work in a world in which God has already been active (for hours).

10 Amy Sherman, *Kingdom Calling: Vocational Stewardship for the Common Good* (Downers Grove, IL: InterVarsity Press), 16.

11 Sherman, *Kingdom Calling*, 34.

12 Daniel Hill, *White Awake: An Honest Look at What It Means to Be White* (Downers Grove, IL: InterVarsity Press, 2017), 22.

13 https://www.communicationtheory.org/the-johari-window-model/
https://www.vistage.com/research-center/business-leadership/strategic-communications/an-introduction-to-the-johari-window/.

14 Brené Brown, PhD, MSW, *Rising Strong: How the Ability to Reset Transforms the Way We Live, Love, Parent, and Lead* (New York: Random House, 2017).

15 Brennan Manning, *Ragamuffin Gospel: Good News for the Bedraggled, Beat-Up, and Burnt Out* (New York: Multnomah, 2005), 25.

16 Kristi Hedges, "Do You Feel Lonely as a Leader? Study Says You're Not Alone," February 23, 2012, *Forbes*, https://www.forbes.com/sites/work-in-progress/2012/02/23/if-mark-zuckerberg-is-lonely-heres-my-solution/?sh=5f79057e37c4.

17 Chibuike Oguh, "Blackstone to Acquire Ancestry.com for $4.7 billion," August 24, 2020, Reuters, https://www.reuters.com/article/us-ancestry-m-a-blackstonegroup/blackstone-to-acquire-ancestry-com-for-4-7-billion-idUSKBN25K0R4.

18 Erin Blakemore, "How the GI Bill's Promise Was Denied to a Million Black WWII Veterans," June 21, 2023, https://www.history.com/news/gi-bill-black-wwii-veterans-benefits.

19 Brookings Institute, https://www.brookings.edu/articles/the-black-white-wealth-gap-left-black-households-more-vulnerable/.

20 Bailey Reiners, "Unconscious Bias: 16 Examples and How to Avoid Them in the Workplace," June 13, 2023, https://builtin.com/diversity-inclusion/unconscious-bias-examples.

21 The Implicit Association Test can be found at https://implicit.harvard.edu/implicit/takeatest.html.

22 Quality of Life Index by City 2023 Mid-Y, https://www.numbeo.com/quality-of-life/rankings.jsp.

23 Emily Badger, Quoctrung Bui, and Robert Gebeloff, "The Neighborhood Is Mostly Black. The Home Buyers Are Mostly White." New York Times, April 27, 2019, https://www.nytimes.com/interactive/2019/04/27/upshot/diversity-housing-maps-raleigh-gentrification.html.

24 The Equal Opportunity Project, http://www.equality-of-opportunity.org/neighborhoods/.

25 http://bulletin-archive.kenyon.edu/x4280.html

26 Stuart Smalley, Wikipedia, https://en.wikipedia.org/wiki/Stuart_Smalley.

27 The word is not spelled the same way—it's generally written Spic—but it sounds the same.

28 U.S. Department of Health and Human Services, Infant Mortality and African Americans https://minorityhealth.hhs.gov/omh/browse.aspx?lvl=4&lvlid=23.

29 National Institutes of Health, https://www.ncbi.nlm.nih.gov/pmc/articles/PMC6381592/#:~:text=Non%2DHispanic%20black%20women%20have,explained%20solely%20by%20sociodemographic%20factors.

30 American Psychological Association, "For Black students infarly harsh discipline can lead to lower grades," https://www.apa.org/news/press/releases/2021/10/black-students-harsh-discipline#:~:text=Overall%2C%20the%20researchers%20found%20that,a%20cell%20phone%20in%20class.

31 Pew Research Center, https://www.pewresearch.org/short-reads/2013/08/21/through-good-times-and-bad-black-unemployment-is-consistently-double-that-of-whites/

32 Annie E. Casey Foundation, https://www.aecf.org/blog/us-foster-care-population-by-race-and-ethnicity#:~:text=In%202021%2C%20Black%20children%20represented,all%20kids%20in%20foster%20care.

33 New York University, https://www.nyu.edu/about/news-publications/news/2020/may/black-drivers-more-likely-to-be-stopped-by-police.html.

34 Pew Charitable Trusts, https://www.pewtrusts.org/en/research-and-analysis/issue-briefs/2023/05/racial-disparities-persist-in-many-us-jails.

35 Brookings Institute, https://www.brookings.edu/articles/the-black-white-wealth-gap-left-black-households-more-vulnerable/.

36 PBS, *Bacon's Rebellion, Class, and Race,* https://pbsnc.pbslearningmedia.org/resource/ush22-soc-baconsrebellion/bacons-rebellion-class-and-race-interactive/.

37 Racial Equity Institute.

38 Equal Justice Initiative, https://eji.org.

39 If you're still trying to keep the "race" and "ethnicity" examples in mind here, these two nations provide slightly different histories. In Rwanda, the genocide was more ethnic, with two warring groups of different ethnic and linguistic backgrounds. In Germany, the genocide was more racial, with blurry and often arbitrary designations for what made someone "Jew" or "not Jew."

40https://journeys.dartmouth.edu/censushistory/2016/10/31/black-and-white-veterans-and-the-gi-bill/.

41http://www.vocativ.com/underworld/drugs/crack-vs-coke-sentencing/index.html.

42https://www.nytimes.com/2016/12/04/nyregion/new-york-prisons-inmates-parole-race.html.

43https://www.census.gov/content/dam/Census/library/visualizations/2021/demo/p60-273/Figure8.pdf;https://www.worldbank.org/en/news/press-release/2018/10/17/nearly-half-the-world-lives-on-less-than-550-a-day.

44https://www.unicef.org/social-policy/child-poverty#:~:text=Across%20the%20world%2C%20about%201,poverty%20due%20to%20COVID%2D19.

45 https://www.federalregister.gov/documents/2022/01/21/2022-01166/annual-update-of-the-hhs-poverty-guidelines, Accessed June 30, 2023.

46 https://www.census.gov/content/dam/Census/library/visualizations/2021/demo/p60-273/Figure8.pdf. To be clear, I'm not necessarily condemning the federal government for this. Legally and logistically, these lines have to be drawn somewhere. My point here is simply to show that poverty statistics in the United States need to be read in their full context.

47 https://www.epi.org/resources/budget/. Accessed June 30, 2023.

48 Brian Fikkert and Steve Corbett, *When Helping Hurts: How to Alleviate Poverty Without Hurting the Poor . . . and Yourself* (Chicago: Moody Press, 2014).

49 Timothy Keller, *Generous Justice: How God's Grace Makes Us Just* (New York: Penguin Books, 2012), 94.

50 Fikkert and Corbett, *When Helping Hurts*, 59.

51 *When Helping Hurts*, 78.

52 "Social Justice at Work: Bringing 'Shalom' into the Workplace, https://www.theologyofwork.org/the-high-calling/blog/social-justice-work-bringing-shalom-workplace.

53 Andrew Julian, "Five Tampa Bay Rays players decline to wear LGBTQ+ logo on uniform during Pride Night celebration," June 7, 2022, https://www.cbssports.com/mlb/news/five-tampa-bay-rays-players-decline-to-wear-lgbtq-logo-on-uniform-during-pride-night-celebration/.

54 Here are just a few: Is God Anti-Gay, Sam Alberry; What God Has to Say about Our Bodies, Sam Alberry; Love into Light, Peter Hubbard; Understanding Sexual Identity, Mark Yarhouse.

55 I recognize that much more than any other part of this conversation, the "trans"element of LGBTQ+ discussions is the most rapidly changing. Leaders will need great wisdom here, since the surrounding conversations (and legal realities) are different from year to year—or even from month to month. I've tried, in this chapter to use examples of transgender individuals and the unique challenges for them in the workplace. But I also know that if I were writing this chapter again in a few years, I would most likely have to update the examples.

56 Crouch's book is well worth reading in its entirety: *Playing God: Redeeming the Gift of Power* (Westmont, IL: Intervarsity Press, 2013).

57 https://www.gallup.com/394373/indicator-employee-engagement.aspx.

58 Jennifer Robison, "Turning Around Employee Turnover," May 8, 2008, https://news.gallup.com/businessjournal/106912/turning-around-your-turnover-problem.aspx.

59 https://www.ccl.org/articles/white-papers/trust-critical-team-success/.

60 Brigid Schulte, "Is Your Work Killing You?", *Slate* magazine, April 24, 2018, https://slate.com/human-interest/2018/04/is-your-work-killing-you.html.

61 Derek Thompson, "The Religion of Workism Is Making Americans Miserable," The Atlantic, February 2019; https://www.theatlantic.com/ideas/archive/2019/02/religion-workism-making-americans-miserable/583441/.

62 Anne Helen Peterson, "How Millennials Became the Burnout Generation," Buzzfeed, January 5, 2019; https://www.buzzfeednews.com/article/annehelenpetersen/millennials-burnout-generation-debt-work. See also Peterson's book, *Can't Even: How Millennials Became the Burnout Generation* (Boston: Mariner Books, 2020).

63https://www.gallup.com/workplace/356063/gallup-q12-employee-engagement-survey.aspx.

64 https://www.aihr.com/blog/job-characteristics-model/.

65 Becca McNeel, "Some Christian Schools Are Finally Grappling with Their Racist

Past and Segregated Present," August 6, 2020, The Hechinger Report, https://hechingerreport.org/christian-schools-grapple-with-demographic-change-and-their-racist-past/.

66 David Brooks, *The Second Mountain: The Quest for a Moral Life* (New York: Random House, 2019).

67 Racial Equity Institute, The Groundwater Approach, April 2, 2019, https://www.prnewswire.com/news-releases/racial-equity-institute-releases-groundwater-approach-whitepaper-to-educate-organizations-about-systemic-racism-300823007.html.

68 Martin Luther King Jr., *Where Do We Go From Here? Chaos or Community* (Boston: Beacon Press, 1967).

69 https://writingexplained.org/systemic-vs-systematic-difference.

70 Dr. Martin Luther King Jr., Speech at Illinois Wesleyan University, 1966, https://www.iwu.edu/mlk/.

ABOUT THE AUTHOR

David Spickard is husband to Alice and dad to his adult children, Ben, Scott, Meg, and Claire. He is the founder and CEO of 11 Ten Leadership, a leadership development company based in Raleigh, North Carolina. Before that, he served as the CEO of Jobs for Life, a global nonprofit organization committed to helping men and women experience the dignity of work.

There are very few sports he does not like, and he is widely known for his (soon to be award-winning) chocolate chip cookies.